Basic Category Theory
for Computer Scientists

Foundations of Computing
Michael Garey and Albert Meyer, editors

Basic Category Theory
for Computer Scientists

Benjamin C. Pierce

The MIT Press
Cambridge, Massachusetts
London, England

This book was typeset by the author using TEX 3.0 and converted to PostScript using Y&Y's DVIPSONE™. Camera-ready copy was produced by Chiron, Inc.

Library of Congress Cataloging-in-Publication Data

Pierce, Benjamin C.
  Basic category theory for computer scientists / Benjamin C. Pierce.
    p.   cm. — (Foundations of computing)
  Includes bibliographical references and index.
  ISBN 978-0-262-66071-6 (pb. : alk. paper)
  1. Computer science—Mathematics. 2. Categories (Mathematics) I. Title. II. Series.
QA76.9.M35P54 1991
511.3—dc20   91-8489
                                                                    CIP

To Roger, Alexandra, and Jessica

Contents

Series Foreword

Theoretical computer science has now undergone several decades of development. The "classical" topics of automata theory, formal languages, and computational complexity have become firmly established, and their importance to other theoretical work and to practice is widely recognized. Stimulated by technological advances, theoreticians have been rapidly expanding the areas under study, and the time delay between theoretical progress and its practical impact has been decreasing dramatically. Much publicity has been given recently to breakthroughs in cryptography and linear programming, and steady progress is being made on programming language semantics, computational geometry, and efficient data structures. Newer, more speculative, areas of study include relational databases, VLSI theory, and parallel and distributed computation. As this list of topics continues expanding, it is becoming more and more difficult to stay abreast of the progress that is being made and increasingly important that the most significant work be distilled and communicated in a manner that will facilitate further research and application of this work. By publishing comprehensive books and specialized monographs on the theoretical aspects of computer science, the series on Foundations of Computing provides a forum in which important research topics can be presented in their entirety and placed in perspective for researchers, students, and practitioners alike.

Michael R. Garey
Albert R. Meyer

Preface

> What we are probably seeking is a "purer" view of functions: a
> theory of functions in themselves, not a theory of functions de-
> rived from sets. What, then, is a pure theory of functions? Answer:
> category theory.
>
> — Scott [104, p. 406]

Category theory is a relatively young branch of pure mathematics, stem-
ming from an area—algebraic topology—that most computer scientists
would consider esoteric. Yet its influence is being felt in many parts
of computer science, including the design of functional and imperative
programming languages, implementation techniques for functional languages, semantic models of programming languages, models of concurrency, type theory, polymorphism, specification languages, constructive
logic, automata theory, and the development of algorithms.

The breadth of this list underscores an important point: category theory is not specialized to a particular setting. It is a basic conceptual and
notational framework in the same sense as set theory or graph theory,
though it deals in more abstract constructions and requires somewhat
heavier notation. The cost of its generality is that category-theoretic
formulations of concepts can be more difficult to grasp than their coun-
terparts in other formalisms; the benefit is that concepts may be dealt
with at a higher level and hidden commonalities allowed to emerge.

Recent issues of theoretical computer science journals give ample
evidence that category theory is already an important tool in some parts
of the field. In a few areas—notably domain theory and semantics—it
is now a standard language of discourse. Fortunately for the beginner,
most computer science research papers draw only on the notation and
some relatively elementary results of category theory. The ADJ group,
early proponents of category theory in computer science, sound a reas-
suring note in the introduction to one of their papers [116]: "...do not
succumb to a feeling that you must understand *all* of category theory before you put it to use. When one talks of a 'set theoretic' model for some
computing phenomenon, [one] is not thinking of a formulation in terms
of measurable cardinals! Similarly, a category theoretic model does not
necessarily involve the Kan extension theorem or double categories."

The first drafts of this book were written while I was studying category theory myself, as background for graduate research in program-

ming languages. Its aim, therefore, is not to promote a particular point of view about how category theory can be applied in computer science—a task better undertaken by more experienced practitioners—but simply to orient the reader in the fundamental vocabulary and synthesize the explanations and intuitions that were most helpful to me on a first encounter with the material.

The tutorial in Chapters 1 and 2 should provide a thorough enough treatment of basic category theory that the reader will feel prepared to approach current research papers applying category theory to computer science or proceed to more advanced texts—for example, the excellent new books by Asperti and Longo [2] and Barr and Wells [5]—for deeper expositions of specific areas. It covers essential notation and constructions and a few more advanced topics (notably adjoints) that are sometimes skipped in short introductions to the subject but are relevant to an appreciation of the field. Chapter 3 illustrates the concepts presented in the tutorial with a sketch of the connection between cartesian closed categories and λ-calculi, an application in the design of programming languages, a summary of work in categorical models of programming language semantics, and a detailed description of some category-theoretic tools for the solution of recursive domain equations. Chapter 4 briefly surveys some of the available textbooks, introductory articles, reference works, and research articles on category theory applied to computer science. A summary of notation and an index appear at the end.

This book could not have been written without the encouragement and generous assistance of my teachers, colleagues, and friends. I am especially grateful to Nico Habermann for suggesting the project; to DEC Systems Research Center, Carnegie Mellon University, and the Office of Naval Research for support while it was underway; to Rod Burstall, Luca Cardelli, Peter Freyd, Robert Harper, Giuseppe Longo, Simone Martini, Gordon Plotkin, John Reynolds, and Dana Scott for informative conversations about its subject matter; to Bob Prior at MIT Press for patient editorial advice; and to Lorrie LeJeune for efficient handling of the manuscript. Comments and suggestions from Martín Abadi, Penny Anderson, Violetta Cavalli-Sforza, Scott Dietzen, Conal Elliott, Andrzej Filinski, Susan Finger, Robert Goldblatt, John Greiner, Nico Habermann, Robert Harper, Nevin Heintze, Dinesh Katiyar, Peter Lee, Mark Maimone, Spiro Michaylov, Frank Pfenning, David Plaut, John Reynolds, Dwight Spencer, Robert Tennent, James Thatcher, Todd Wilson, Elizabeth Wolf, and two anonymous referees greatly improved my presentation of the material and eliminated a number of errors in previous drafts.

Finally, I am pleased to acknowledge a huge debt to the labors of other authors, particularly to Robert Goldblatt [40], Saunders Mac Lane [67], and David Rydeheard [95,96,98]. Their books, foremost among many others, were frequent guides in the choice of examples and exercises, organization of material, and proper presentation of the subject's "folklore." There are a few points—marked in the text—where I have closely followed the structure of a particularly beautiful presentation of a concept by another author. Errors in these sections, as in the rest of the text, are of course solely my responsibility.

Pittsburgh, Pennsylvania
January 25, 1991

1 Basic Constructions

This chapter and the following one present a brief tutorial on basic concepts of category theory. The goals of the tutorial are, first, to be complete enough to prepare the reader for more difficult textbooks and research papers applying category theory in computer science; second, to cover important topics in sufficient depth that the reader comes away with some sense of the contribution of category theory to mathematical thinking; and third, to be reasonably short. Most sections begin with a rigorous definition, prefaced with an informal explanation of the construction and followed by examples and exercises illustrating its use in various contexts.

1.1 Categories

We begin by defining the notion of category and presenting a variety of examples from computer science and algebra.

1.1.1 Definition A **category C** comprises:

1. a collection of **objects**;

2. a collection of **arrows** (often called **morphisms**);

3. operations assigning to each arrow f an object $dom\ f$, its **domain**, and an object $cod\ f$, its **codomain** (we write $f : A \to B$ or $A \xrightarrow{f} B$ to show that $dom\ f = A$ and $cod\ f = B$; the collection of all arrows with domain A and codomain B is written $\mathbf{C}(A, B)$);

4. a composition operator assigning to each pair of arrows f and g, with $cod\ f = dom\ g$, a **composite** arrow $g \circ f : dom\ f \to cod\ g$, satisfying the following *associative law*:

    for any arrows $f : A \to B$, $g : B \to C$, and $h : C \to D$ (with A, B, C, and D not necessarily distinct),

    $$h \circ (g \circ f) = (h \circ g) \circ f;$$

5. for each object A, an **identity** arrow $id_A : A \to A$ satisfying the following *identity law*:

    for any arrow $f : A \to B$,

    $$id_B \circ f = f \quad \text{and} \quad f \circ id_A = f.$$

1.1.2 Remark   Categories are defined here in terms of ordinary set theory. "Collections" are just sets, or occasionally proper classes, since we want to talk about things like the "collection of all sets," which is too big to be a set. "Operations" are set-theoretic functions. "Equality" is set-theoretic identity.

Our first example, an important source of intuition throughout the tutorial, is the category whose objects are sets and whose arrows are functions. There is no circularity here: we are not *defining* sets in terms of categories, but merely *presenting* a well-known mathematical domain as a category.

1.1.3 Example   The category **Set** has sets as objects and total functions between sets as arrows. Composition of arrows is set-theoretic function composition. Identity arrows are identity functions.

To see that **Set** is a category, let us restate its definition in the same format as Definition 1.1.1 and check that the laws hold:

1. An object in **Set** is a set.

2. An arrow $f : A \to B$ in **Set** is a total function from the set A into the set B.

3. For each total function f with domain A and codomain B, we have *dom* $f = A$, *cod* $f = B$, and $f \in \mathbf{Set}(A, B)$.

4. The composition of a total function $f : A \to B$ with another total function $g : B \to C$ is the total function from A to C mapping each element $a \in A$ to $g(f(a)) \in C$. Composition of total functions on sets is associative: for any functions $f : A \to B$, $g : B \to C$, and $h : C \to D$, we have $h \circ (g \circ f) = (h \circ g) \circ f$.

5. For each set A, the identity function id_A is a total function with domain and codomain A. For any function $f : A \to B$, the identity functions on A and B satisfy the equations required by the identity law: $id_B \circ f = f$ and $f \circ id_A = f$.

1.1.4 Remark   There is one subtlety in the definition of the category **Set**: each function on sets corresponds to many arrows in **Set**. For example, the function that takes every real number r to r^2 maps elements of R (the set of real numbers) into elements of R, and hence corresponds to an arrow $s : \mathsf{R} \to \mathsf{R}$. But it also maps elements of R into elements of R^+ (the set of nonnegative real numbers), and hence corresponds to an arrow $s' : \mathsf{R} \to \mathsf{R}^+$. These are two *different* arrows of the category **Set**.

To be rigorous, we should define a **Set**-arrow $f : A \to B$ to be a tuple (f, B), where f is a total function with domain A and B is a set containing f's image. Alternatively, we could change the definition of category to allow the sets of arrows between different objects to overlap, giving what is sometimes called a **pre-category** or **naked category.** Some authors favor the latter approach, where notions like "function" have their ordinary mathematical meaning. The cost of this solution is some extra complication in later definitions, e.g., the definition of "functor," arising from the fact that by looking just at an arrow in a pre-category it is not in general possible to tell what its domain and codomain are.

Following the more common practice, we use the first approach in this tutorial, though (also following standard practice) we elide the details of ensuring that sets of arrows are disjoint.

The category laws are so obviously satisfied by **Set** that it may seem as though Definition 1.1.1 is vacuous. The next example shows that there is usually some work to be done in showing that some given collection of objects and arrows form a category. In more complicated examples, the work can be substantial.

1.1.5 Example A *partial ordering* $\leq_P$ on a set P is a reflexive, transitive, and antisymmetric relation on the elements of P—that is, one for which: (1) $p \leq p$, (2) $p \leq p' \leq p''$ implies $p \leq p''$, and (3) $p \leq p'$ and $p' \leq p$ imply $p = p'$, for all $p, p', p'' \in P$. An *order-preserving* (or *monotone*) function from $(P, \leq_P)$ to $(Q, \leq_Q)$ is a function $f : P \to Q$ such that if $p \leq_P p'$ then $f(p) \leq_Q f(p')$.

The category **Poset** has as objects all partially-ordered sets and as arrows all order-preserving total functions.

Let us go once more through the exercise of checking this carefully against Definition 1.1.1:

1. An object in **Poset** is a set P with a reflexive, transitive, antisymmetric relation $\leq_P$ on the elements of P.

2. An arrow $f : (P, \leq_P) \to (Q, \leq_Q)$ in **Poset** is a total function from P into Q that preserves the ordering on P, that is, such that if $p \leq_P p'$ then $f(p) \leq_Q f(p')$.

3. For each total order-preserving function f with domain P and codomain Q, we have $dom\, f = (P, \leq_P)$, $cod\, f = (Q, \leq_Q)$, and $f \in$ **Poset**$((P, \leq_P), (Q, \leq_Q))$.

4. The composition of two total order-preserving functions $f : P \to Q$ and $g : Q \to R$ is a total function $g \circ f$ from P to R. Furthermore, if $p \leq_P p'$ then, since f preserves P's ordering, $f(p) \leq_Q f(p')$; and since g preserves Q's ordering, $g(f(p)) \leq_R g(f(p'))$. So $g \circ f$ is order-preserving. Composition of order-preserving functions is associative because each order-preserving function on partially-ordered sets is

just a function on sets and composition of functions on sets is associative.

5. For each partial order $(P, \leq_P)$, the identity function id_P preserves the ordering on P and satisfies the equations of the identity law.

Another class of familiar algebraic structures, monoids, also forms the basis of a category:

1.1.6 Example   A *monoid* $(M, \cdot, e)$ is an underlying set M equipped with a binary operation $\cdot$ from pairs of elements of M into M such that $(x \cdot y) \cdot z = x \cdot (y \cdot z)$ for all $x, y, z \in M$ and a distinguished element e such that $e \cdot x = x = x \cdot e$ for all $x \in M$. A *monoid homomorphism* from $(M, \cdot, e)$ to $(M', \cdot', e')$ is a function $f : M \rightarrow M'$ such that $f(e) = e'$ and $f(x \cdot y) = f(x) \cdot' f(y)$. The composition of two monoid homomorphisms is the same as their composition as functions on sets.

The category **Mon** has monoids as objects and monoid homomorphisms as arrows. The verification that **Mon** is actually a category follows exactly the same steps as for **Poset**; it is easy to check that composing two functions that are both homomorphisms gives a homomorphism.

More abstractly, the algebras with a given signature Ω form the objects of a category:

1.1.7 Example Let Ω be a set of operator symbols, equipped with a mapping ar from elements of Ω to natural numbers; for each $\omega \in \Omega$, $ar(\omega)$ is the *arity* of ω. An Ω-*algebra* A is a set $|A|$ (the *carrier* of A) and, for each operator ω of arity $ar(\omega)$, a function $a_\omega : |A|^{ar(\omega)} \rightarrow |A|$, called the *interpretation* of ω, mapping $ar(\omega)$-tuples of elements of the carrier back into the carrier. An Ω-*homomorphism* from an Ω-algebra A to an Ω-algebra B is a function $h : |A| \rightarrow |B|$ such that for each operator $\omega \in \Omega$ and tuple $x_1, x_2 \ldots, x_{ar(\omega)}$ of elements of $|A|$, the following equation holds:

$$h(a_\omega(x_1, x_2, \ldots, x_{ar(\omega)})) = b_\omega(h(x_1), h(x_2), \ldots, h(x_{ar(\omega)})).$$

The category Ω-**Alg** has Ω-algebras as objects and Ω-homomorphisms as arrows.

This construction can be refined by adding to the signature Ω a set E of *equations* between expressions built from elements of Ω and a set $\{x, y, z, \ldots\}$ of variable symbols. Then the Ω-algebras A for which the equations in E are satisfied under all assignments of elements of $|A|$ to the variable symbols form the objects of a category $(\Omega, \mathbf{E})$-**Alg**. For example, if

$$
\begin{aligned}
\Omega &= \{\cdot, e\} \\
ar(\cdot) &= 2 \\
ar(e) &= 0 \\
E &= \{(x \cdot y) \cdot z = x \cdot (y \cdot z),\ e \cdot x = x,\ x \cdot e = x\}
\end{aligned}
$$

then (Ω, E)-**Alg** is another name for **Mon**.

The objects in all of these categories can be viewed as "sets with structure" and the arrows as "structure preserving maps"; such categories are called **concrete**. From this perspective, it is easy to see why category theory is often described as a generalization of universal algebra [41], which studies the common properties of algebraic structures. The following table lists a few more categories that fit this intuition:

Category	Objects	Arrows
Set	sets	total functions
Pfn	sets	partial functions
FinSet	finite sets	finite total functions
Mon	monoids	monoid homomorphisms
Poset	posets	monotone functions
Grp	groups	group homomorphisms
Ω-**Alg**	algebras with signature Ω	Ω-homomorphisms
CPO	complete partial orders	continuous functions
Vect	vector spaces	linear transforms
Met	metric spaces	contraction maps
Top	topological spaces	continuous functions

The concrete categories form an important class, but there are many other interesting categories. For example, here are a few useful *finite* categories:

1.1.8 Example The category **0** has no objects and no arrows. The identity and associativity laws are vacuously satisfied.

1.1.9 Example The category **1** has one object and one arrow. By the identity law, the arrow must be the identity for the object. The composition of this arrow with itself can only be itself, which satisfies the identity and associativity laws. Note that we didn't bother to specify what mathematical or physical entities the object and arrow are intended to represent. What matters here is only their algebraic properties, and these are fully determined by the category laws.

1.1.10 Example The category **2** has two objects, two identity arrows, and an arrow from one object to the other. Again, it doesn't matter what the objects and arrows represent, but to make it easier to talk about them we might call the objects A and B and the non-identity arrow f. There is only one way to define composition; it is then easy to check that the identity and associativity laws are satisfied.

1.1.11 Example The category **3** has three objects (call them A, B, and C), three identity arrows, and three other arrows: $f : A \to B$, $g : B \to C$, and $h : A \to C$. Again, composition can be defined in only one way and both category laws are satisfied.

Note that since f, g, and h are the only non-identity arrows of **3**, it must be the case that $g \circ f = h$.

The categories **2** and **3** might be displayed graphically like this:

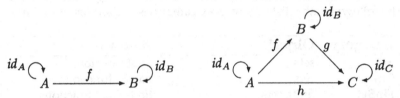

A different sort of category is obtained by considering an *individual* algebraic structure as a category.

1.1.12 Example A partially ordered set $(P, \leq)$ gives rise to a category whose objects are the elements of P. Between each pair of objects p and p' with $p \leq p'$, there is a single arrow representing this fact; there is no arrow from p to p' when $p \not\leq p'$. Composition of arrows is clearly associative, since there is at most one arrow between any given pair of objects. The identity law now corresponds to the reflexivity condition for partial orders, while the existence of composite arrows corresponds to transitivity. The antisymmetry condition is not required: in fact, every *preorder* (that is, every set P with a transitive and reflexive relation $\leq$) gives rise to a category.

If we regard partially ordered sets as categories, then **Poset** is an example of a category of categories.

1.1.13 Example A monoid $(M, \cdot, e)$ may be represented as a category with a single object. The elements of M are represented as arrows from this object to itself, the identity element e is represented as the identity arrow, and the operation $\cdot$ is represented as composition of arrows. Conversely, any category with a single object gives rise to a monoid.

We will omit checking the category axioms from this point on. However, the reader is encouraged to continue to do so.

Many branches of mathematics besides algebra have proved amenable to categorical treatment. Of particular interest to computer science is the field of **categorical logic**, which arises from the following observation:

1.1.14 Example   By a twist of perspective, we can call the objects in an arbitrary category *formulas* and the arrows *proofs*. An arrow $f : A \to B$ is viewed as a proof of the logical implication $A \supset B$. In particular, the identity arrow $id_A : A \to A$ is an instance of the reflexivity axiom, and the composition of arrows

$$\frac{f : A \to B \quad g : B \to C}{g \circ f : A \to C}$$

is a rule of inference asserting the transitivity of implication. (Several of the books discussed in Chapter 4 are concerned with this point of view.)

Another fruitful point of view takes the objects of a category to be the *types* of a functional programming language:

1.1.15 Example   Consider a simple functional language with primitive types

Int	integers
Real	reals
Bool	truth values
Unit	a one-element type,

built-in operations

iszero : *Int* $\to$ *Bool*	test for zero
not : *Bool* $\to$ *Bool*	negation
succ$_{Int}$: *Int* $\to$ *Int*	integer successor
succ$_{Real}$: *Real* $\to$ *Real*	real successor
toReal : *Int* $\to$ *Real*	integer to real conversion,

and constants

zero : *Int*
true : *Bool*
false : *Bool*
unit : *Unit*.

The corresponding category **FPL** is built by

1. taking *Int*, *Real*, *Bool*, and *Unit* to be objects;

2. taking *iszero*, *not*, *succ*$_{Int}$, *succ*$_{Real}$, and *toReal* to be arrows;

3. taking the constants *zero*, *true*, *false*, and *unit* to be arrows from the *Unit* object to *Int*, *Bool*, *Bool*, and *Unit*, respectively, which map the single element of *Unit* to the appropriate elements of these types;

4. adding arrows for the identity functions at each type;

5. for every composable pair of arrows, adding an arrow for the function formed by composing them;

6. equating certain arrows, such as *false = not∘true* and *iszero∘zero = true*, that represent the same functions according to the semantics of the language.

Leaving out the identities and composites, the category **FPL** looks like this:

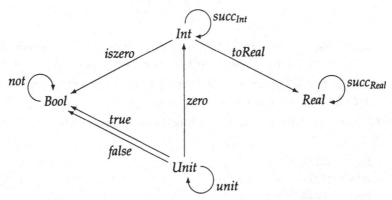

This simple example omits many features of modern functional programming languages. Most functional languages allow functions to be passed as parameters to other functions and returned as results of functions; the machinery needed to model such languages as categories is developed in Section 1.10. Parameterized data types and polymorphic functions, also common features in modern functional languages, are addressed in Section 2.3.

In addition to categories of mathematical objects from other domains, there are many ways in which categories can be built up from other categories.

1.1.16 Example   For each category **C**, the objects of the **dual category** **C**ᵒᵖ are the same as those of **C**; the arrows in **C**ᵒᵖ are the opposites of the arrows in **C**. That is, if $f : A \rightarrow B$ is a arrow of **C** then $f : B \rightarrow A$ is a arrow of **C**ᵒᵖ. Composite and identity arrows are defined in the obvious way.

Each of the definitions of category theory can be restated "with arrows reversed" as a definition in the dual category. In fact, most definitions come in pairs—product/coproduct, equalizer/coequalizer, monomorphism/epimorphism, pullback/pushout—with a "co-x" in a category **C** being the same thing as an "x" in **C**ᵒᵖ.

Moreover, any statement S about categories can be transformed into a dual statement S^{op} by exchanging the words "domain" and "codomain" and replacing each composite $g \circ f$ by $f \circ g$. If S is true of a category $\mathbf{C}$, then by definition S^{op} is true of $\mathbf{C}^{op}$. If S is true of *all* categories, then because every category is the opposite of its opposite, S^{op} is also true of all categories. This observation, often called the **duality principle**, is a convenient source of "free theorems" about categories: once a theorem is proved, its dual follows immediately.

1.1.17 Example For any pair of categories $\mathbf{C}$ and $\mathbf{D}$, the **product category** $\mathbf{C} \times \mathbf{D}$ has as objects pairs (A, B) of a $\mathbf{C}$-object A and a $\mathbf{D}$-object B and as arrows pairs (f, g) of a $\mathbf{C}$-arrow f and a $\mathbf{D}$-arrow g. Composition and identity arrows are defined pairwise: $(f, g) \circ (h, i) = (f \circ h, g \circ i)$ and $id_{(A, B)} = (id_A, id_B)$.

1.1.18 Example (This is a more involved example, included to give some practice with the abstract manipulation sometimes required to follow categorical arguments. Try checking the category axioms with pencil and paper.)

$\mathbf{Set}^{\rightarrow}$ is the **category of arrows** of $\mathbf{Set}$. The objects of $\mathbf{Set}^{\rightarrow}$ are exactly the arrows in $\mathbf{Set}$—that is, each $\mathbf{Set}$-arrow $f : A \rightarrow B$ is an *object* in $\mathbf{Set}^{\rightarrow}$. This means that an arrow in $\mathbf{Set}^{\rightarrow}$ has $\mathbf{Set}$-arrows as its domain and codomain; a $\mathbf{Set}^{\rightarrow}$-arrow from $f : A \rightarrow B$ to $f' : A' \rightarrow B'$ is defined to be a pair (a, b) of $\mathbf{Set}$-arrows $a : A \rightarrow A'$ and $b : B \rightarrow B'$ such that $f' \circ a = b \circ f$. The composition of the $\mathbf{Set}^{\rightarrow}$-arrows

$$(a, b) : (f : A \rightarrow B) \rightarrow (f' : A' \rightarrow B')$$

and

$$(a', b') : (f' : A' \rightarrow B') \rightarrow (f'' : A'' \rightarrow B'')$$

is defined to be $(a', b') \circ (a, b) = (a' \circ a, b' \circ b)$.

For each category $\mathbf{C}$ we can define the category of **arrows over $\mathbf{C}$** by substituting $\mathbf{C}$ for $\mathbf{Set}$ above.

Finally, we can define the subcategories of a category $\mathbf{C}$:

1.1.19 Definition A category $\mathbf{B}$ is a **subcategory** of $\mathbf{C}$ if

1. each object of $\mathbf{B}$ is an object of $\mathbf{C}$;
2. for all $\mathbf{B}$-objects B and B', $\mathbf{B}(B, B') \subseteq \mathbf{C}(B, B')$; and
3. composites and identity arrows are the same in $\mathbf{B}$ as in $\mathbf{C}$.

1.1.20 Exercises

1. Show how an arbitrary set can be considered as a category, following Example 1.1.12.

2. A group $(G, \cdot, ^{-1}, e)$ is a set G equipped with a binary operation $\cdot$, a unary operation $^{-1}$, and a distinguished element e such that:

 (a) $(x \cdot y) \cdot z = x \cdot (y \cdot z)$ for all x, y, and z in G;

 (b) $e \cdot x = x = x \cdot e$ for all x in G;

 (c) $x \cdot x^{-1} = e = x^{-1} \cdot x$ for all x in G.

Show how an arbitrary group can be considered as a category, following Example 1.1.13.

3. Verify that each of the categories **0**, **1**, **2**, and **3** corresponds to a partial order. What would the category **4** look like? The category **5**? The category **N** with an object corresponding to each natural number?

4. Complete the following specification of the category **M** and verify the laws of Definition 1.1.1:

 (a) the objects of **M** are the natural numbers;

 (b) an **M**-arrow $f : m \to n$ is an m-by-n matrix of real numbers;

 (c) the composite $g \circ f$ of two arrows $f : m \to n$ and $g : n \to p$ is the matrix product of f and g.

5. Redraw the diagram in Example 1.1.15 so that it shows all the distinct arrows of **FPL**. When two arrows are equated according to step 6 of the construction of **FPL**, a single arrow with both labels should appear in the drawing. (There are infinitely many arrows between some pairs of objects, so you'll need to abbreviate in some cases.)

1.1.21 Historical Note   According to Mac Lane [67, pp. 29-30], the fundamental idea of representing a function by an arrow first appeared in topology around 1940, probably in the work of Hurewicz (c.f. [53]). Commutative diagrams (Section 1.2 below) were probably also first used by Hurewicz. Categories, functors (Section 2.1), and natural transformations (Section 2.3) were discovered by Eilenberg and Mac Lane [22]. A direct treatment of categories in their own right appeared in 1945 [23]. The word "category" was borrowed from Aristotle and Kant, "functor" from Carnap, and "natural transformation" from the informal practice of the time.

1.2   Diagrams

The last few examples of Section 1.1 show how descriptions of categories and statements about objects and arrows within them can quickly become complicated, especially when they involve conditions like "$f' \circ a = b \circ f$" as in Example 1.1.18. To make such descriptions and the arguments involving them more manageable, category theorists often use a graphical style of presentation.

1.2.1 Definition A **diagram** in a category **C** is a collection of vertices and directed edges, consistently labeled with objects and arrows of **C**, where "consistently" means that if an edge in the diagram is labeled with an arrow f and f has domain A and codomain B, then the endpoints of this edge must be labeled with A and B.

(These diagrams *in* categories are not to be confused with the diagrams *of* categories in Section 1.1.)

Diagrams are often used for stating and proving properties of categorical constructions. Such properties can often be expressed by saying that a particular diagram commutes:

1.2.2 Definition A diagram in a category **C** is said to **commute** if, for every pair of vertices X and Y, all the paths in the diagram from X to Y are equal, in the sense that each path in the diagram determines an arrow and these arrows are equal in **C**. For example, saying that "the diagram

$$
\begin{array}{ccc}
X & \xrightarrow{\;\;f'\;\;} & Z \\
{\scriptstyle g'}\big\downarrow & & \big\downarrow{\scriptstyle g} \\
W & \xrightarrow[\;\;f\;\;]{} & Y
\end{array}
$$

commutes" is exactly the same as saying that $f \circ g' = g \circ f'$.

A useful (but not universally accepted) refinement of this convention is to require that two paths be equal only when at least one of them contains more than one arrow. Thus the commutativity of the diagram

$$
X \underset{g}{\overset{f}{\rightrightarrows}} Y \xrightarrow{\;\;h\;\;} Z
$$

implies that $h \circ f = h \circ g$, but not that $f = g$.

Example 1.1.18 can now be restated in a much more comprehensible form:

1.2.3 Example Each **Set**-arrow $f : A \to B$ is an object in the category **Set**$^{\to}$. A **Set**$^{\to}$-arrow from $f : A \to B$ to $f' : A' \to B'$ is a pair (a, b) of

Set-arrows such that the diagram

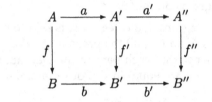

commutes in **Set**. The composition of the **Set**$^\rightarrow$-arrows $(a, b) : (f : A \rightarrow B) \rightarrow (f' : A' \rightarrow B')$ and $(a', b') : (f' : A' \rightarrow B') \rightarrow (f'' : A'' \rightarrow B'')$ is $(a', b') \circ (a, b) = (a' \circ a, b' \circ b)$, which corresponds to the diagram formed by "pasting together" two copies of the first one:

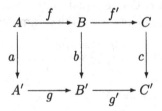

When a property is stated in terms of commutative diagrams, proofs involving that property can often be given "visually." The following simple proof demonstrates the technique; observe that the equations correspond to paths in the diagram, and that these paths are transformed by replacing one path through a commuting subdiagram with another.

1.2.4 Proposition If both inner squares of the following diagram commute, then so does the outer rectangle.

$$
\begin{array}{ccccc}
A & \xrightarrow{f} & B & \xrightarrow{f'} & C \\
\downarrow{\scriptstyle a} & & \downarrow{\scriptstyle b} & & \downarrow{\scriptstyle c} \\
A' & \xrightarrow{g} & B' & \xrightarrow{g'} & C'
\end{array}
$$

Proof:

$$
\begin{aligned}
(g' \circ g) \circ a &= g' \circ (g \circ a) &&\text{(associativity)} \\
&= g' \circ (b \circ f) &&\text{(commutativity of first square)} \\
&= (g' \circ b) \circ f &&\text{(associativity)} \\
&= (c \circ f') \circ f &&\text{(commutativity of second square)} \\
&= c \circ (f' \circ f) &&\text{(associativity).}
\end{aligned}
$$

(*End of Proof*)

1.2.5 Remark Some authors, especially computer scientists, prefer to notate composites in *diagrammatic* rather than *functional* order, writing "$f ; g$" instead of "$g \circ f$" so that when expressions are read from left to right the arrows occur in the same order as in the diagram. The notation given in Definition 1.1.1, though less convenient for computer science applications, is more common in the category theory literature and will be used exclusively in this book.

1.2.6 Remark When a functional language is described as a category, as in Example 1.1.15, commutative diagrams can be used to assert the validity of program transformations in which the order of operations is permuted. For example, asserting the commutativity of the diagram

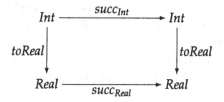

in the category **FPL** is equivalent to stating that the result of converting an integer to a real and then computing its successor is the same as computing its integer successor and converting this to a real. We shall have more to say about this example in Section 3.2.

1.3 Monomorphisms, Epimorphisms, and Isomorphisms

When we reason about sets and functions, we are often interested in functions with special properties such as being injective (one-to-one), surjective (onto), or bijective (defining an isomorphism). Appropriate analogues of these concepts also play an important role in categorical reasoning.

1.3.1 Definition An arrow $f : B \to C$ in a category **C** is a **monomorphism** (or "is **monic**") if, for any pair of **C**-arrows $g : A \to B$ and $h : A \to B$, the equality $f \circ g = f \circ h$ implies that $g = h$.

1.3.2 Proposition In **Set**, the monomorphisms are just the injective functions (the functions f such that $f(x) = f(y)$ implies $x = y$.)

Proof: Let $f : B \to C$ be an injective function, and let $g, h : A \to B$ be such that $f \circ g = f \circ h$ but $g \neq h$. Then there is some element $a \in A$ for which $g(a) \neq h(a)$. But since f is injective, $f(g(a)) \neq f(h(a))$, which contradicts our assumption that $f \circ g = f \circ h$. This shows that f is a monomorphism.

Conversely, let $f : B \to C$ be a monomorphism. If f is not injective, then there are distinct elements $b, b' \in B$ for which $f(b) = f(b')$. Let A be the one-element set $\{a\}$, and let $g : A \to B$ map a to b while $h : A \to B$ maps a to b'. Then $f(g(a)) = f(h(a))$, contradicting the assumption that f is a monomorphism.   (*End of Proof*)

1.3.3 Convention   The category to which an object or arrow belongs is often omitted when it is unimportant or clear from context. We adopt this convention from now on, using explicit qualifications like "C-arrow" only when there would otherwise be a possibility of confusion.

1.3.4 Definition   An arrow $f : A \to B$ is an **epimorphism** (or "is **epic**") if, for any pair of arrows $g : B \to C$ and $h : B \to C$, the equality $g \circ f = h \circ f$ implies that $g = h$.

1.3.5 Proposition   In **Set**, the epimorphisms are just the surjective functions. (A function $f : A \to B$ is surjective if for each $b \in B$ there is an $a \in A$ for which $f(a) = b$.)

The correspondence

$$
\begin{array}{rcl}
\text{mono} & \leftrightarrow & \text{injective} \quad \text{(one-to-one)} \\
\text{epi} & \leftrightarrow & \text{surjective} \quad \text{(onto)}
\end{array}
$$

provides a good mnemonic for remembering the definitions of monomorphisms and epimorphisms: monomorphisms in **Set** are injective, epimorphisms are surjective. But this correspondence does not hold in general. The internal structure of the objects in some concrete categories can be used to construct epimorphisms, for example, that are not surjective when considered as functions on sets:

1.3.6 Example   Both $(\mathsf{Z}, +, 0)$, the monoid of integers under addition, and $(\mathsf{N}, +, 0)$, the monoid of nonnegative integers under addition, are objects of the category **Mon**. The inclusion function $i : (\mathsf{N}, +, 0) \to (\mathsf{Z}, +, 0)$ that maps each nonnegative integer z to the integer z is a monomorphism, as we would expect by analogy with **Set**. But i is also an epimorphism, although it is clearly *not* surjective. To see this, assume that $f \circ i = g \circ i$ for two homomorphisms f and g from $(\mathsf{Z}, +, 0)$ to some monoid $(M, *, E)$. Take any $z \in \mathsf{Z}$. If $z \geq 0$, then it is the image under i of the same z considered as an element of N, so

$$f(z) = f(i(z)) = g(i(z)) = g(z).$$

If $z < 0$, then $-z \geq 0$ and $-z \in \mathbb{N}$; we reason as follows:

$$
\begin{aligned}
f(z) &= f(z) * E \\
&= f(z) * g(0) \\
&= f(z) * g(-z + z) \\
&= f(z) * (g(-z) * g(z)) \\
&= (f(z) * g(-z)) * g(z) \\
&= (f(z) * g(i(-z))) * g(z) \\
&= (f(z) * f(i(-z))) * g(z) \\
&= (f(z) * f(-z)) * g(z) \\
&= f(z + -z) * g(z) \\
&= f(0) * g(z) \\
&= E * g(z) \\
&= g(z).
\end{aligned}
$$

Since $f(z) = g(z)$ for all z, we have $f = g$; so i is an epimorphism.

In category theory, the analogues of injective and surjective functions on sets are not sufficient to describe the full range of special kinds of arrows. Monomorphisms and epimorphisms are very common, but many textbooks define others—retractions, sections, zero arrows, bimorphisms, subobjects, quotient objects, and more. We limit ourselves here to mentioning just one more variety.

1.3.7 Definition An arrow $f : A \to B$ is an **isomorphism** if there is an arrow $f^{-1} : B \to A$, called the *inverse* of f, such that $f^{-1} \circ f = id_A$ and $f \circ f^{-1} = id_B$. The objects A and B are said to be **isomorphic** if there is an isomorphism between them.

1.3.8 Example A group corresponds to a one-object category where every arrow is an isomorphism.

1.3.9 Definition Two objects that are isomorphic are often said to be identical **up to isomorphism** or **within an isomorphism**. Similarly, an object A with some property P is said to be "unique up to isomorphism" if every object satisfying P is isomorphic to A.

In fact, identity and uniqueness of categorical entities are so commonly "up to isomorphism" that, except in very rigorous arguments, the qualification is often elided.

1.3.10 Exercises

1. Prove Proposition 1.3.5.

2. Show that in any category, if two arrows f and g are both monic then their composition $g \circ f$ is monic. Also, if $g \circ f$ is monic then so is f.

3. Dualize the previous exercise: state and prove the analogous proposition for epics. (Be careful on the second part.)

4. Show that if f is an isomorphism then its inverse f^{-1} is unique.

5. Show that if f^{-1} is the inverse of $f : A \to B$ and g^{-1} is the inverse of $g : B \to C$, then $f^{-1} \circ g^{-1}$ is the inverse of $g \circ f$.

6. Find a category containing an arrow that is both a monomorphism and an epimorphism, but not an isomorphism.

1.4   Initial and Terminal Objects

For the next several sections we will be examining various **universal constructions** in categories. The simplest of these is the notion of initial object and its dual:

1.4.1 Definition An object 0 is called an **initial object** if, for every object A, there is exactly one arrow from 0 to A.

1.4.2 Definition Dually, an object 1 is called a **terminal** or **final object** if, for every object A, there is exactly one arrow from A to 1.

Arrows from an initial object or to a terminal object are often labeled "!" to highlight their uniqueness:

$$A \xrightarrow{\;\;!\;\;} 1$$

1.4.3 Example   In **Set**, the empty set $\{\}$ is the only initial object; for every set S, the empty function is the unique function from $\{\}$ to S. Each one-element set is a terminal object, since for every set S there is a function from S to a one-element set $\{x\}$ mapping every element of S to x, and furthermore this is the only total function from S to $\{x\}$.

1.4.4 Example   In the category Ω-**Alg** of algebras with signature Ω, the initial object is the *initial algebra* (or *term algebra*) whose carrier consists of all finite trees where each node is labeled with an operator from Ω and where each node labeled with ω has exactly $ar(\omega)$ subtrees. (It is easy to see that this defines an Ω-algebra. The initiality of this algebra is a standard result of universal algebra [41].) The unique homomorphism from the term algebra to another Ω-algebra is a *semantic interpretation function*.

1.4.5 Example   Terminal objects can be used to provide a category-theoretic analogue of the *elements* of sets. The motivating observation is that, in the category **Set**, the functions from a singleton set to a set S are in one-to-one correspondence with the elements of S. Moreover, if x is an element of S, considered as an arrow $x : 1 \to S$ from some one-element set 1, and f is a function from S to some other set T, then the element $f(x)$ is the unique element of T that is in the image of the composite function $f \circ x$.

In categorical terms, an arrow from a terminal object to an object S is called a **global element** or **constant** of S.

1.4.6 Exercises

1. Show that terminal objects are unique up to isomorphism, that is, that two terminal objects in the same category must be isomorphic. Use duality to obtain a short proof that any two initial objects are isomorphic.

2. What are the terminal objects in **Set** × **Set**? In **Set**$^{\to}$? In a poset considered as a category? What are the initial objects in these categories?

3. Name a category with no initial objects. Name one with no terminal objects. Name one where the initial and terminal objects are the same.

1.5   Products

The usual set-theoretic definition of the *cartesian product* of two sets A and B is:

$$A \times B = \{(a, b) \mid a \in A \text{ and } b \in B\}.$$

Using the observation of Example 1.4.5 that elements can be treated as arrows from a terminal object, we could perhaps define a categorical product construction with global elements. However, this would be contrary to the style of category theory, which abstracts away from elements, treating objects as black boxes with unexamined internal structure and focusing attention on the properties of arrows *between* objects. What we need is an "arrow-theoretic" characterization of products.

What arrows are particularly relevant to products of sets? When we form a product of two sets A and B we also define *projection functions* $\pi_1 : A \times B \to A$ and $\pi_2 : A \times B \to B$. These functions are so closely linked to the product itself that we can think of the product as actually being the tuple $(A \times B, \pi_1, \pi_2)$. In fact, if we consider the set of all tuples of this form—tuples (X, f_1, f_2) consisting of a set X and two functions $f_1 : X \to A$ and $f_2 : X \to B$—we find that $(A \times B, \pi_1, \pi_2)$ is an *optimal* representative of this set, in the following sense.

Assume that for some set C, there are two functions $f : C \to A$ and $g : C \to B$. Then we can form a *product function* $\langle f, g \rangle : C \to A \times B$, defined by:

$$\langle f, g \rangle(x) = (f(x),\, g(x)).$$

The functions f and g can be recovered from $\langle f, g \rangle$ by setting $f = \pi_1 \circ \langle f, g \rangle$ and $g = \pi_2 \circ \langle f, g \rangle$. Moreover, $\langle f, g \rangle$ is the only function from C to $A \times B$ with this property.

Of course, $(A \times B,\, \pi_1,\, \pi_2)$ is not the only representative of the set of tuples $(X,\, f_1,\, f_2)$ that is optimal in this sense. For example, the tuple $(B \times A,\, \pi_2,\, \pi_1)$ is just as good. But $A \times B$ and $B \times A$ can be placed in one-to-one correspondence—that is, they are the same up to an isomorphism. In categorical terms we think of them as essentially the same.

This motivates a general definition of categorical products. (Note that here we are considering products *within* a category rather than products *of* categories as in Example 1.1.17.)

1.5.1 Definition   A **product** of two objects A and B is an object $A \times B$, together with two **projection arrows** $\pi_1 : A \times B \to A$ and $\pi_2 : A \times B \to B$, such that for any object C and pair of arrows $f : C \to A$ and $g : C \to B$ there is exactly one **mediating arrow** $\langle f, g \rangle : C \to A \times B$ making the diagram

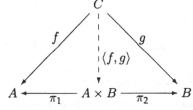

commute—that is, such that $\pi_1 \circ \langle f, g \rangle = f$ and $\pi_2 \circ \langle f, g \rangle = g$.

(Dashed arrows in commutative diagrams are used to represent arrows that are asserted to exist when the rest of the diagram is filled in appropriately.)

1.5.2 Exercise   Show that any object X with arrows $\pi_A : X \to A$ and $\pi_B : X \to B$ satisfying the definition of "X is a product of A and B" is isomorphic to $A \times B$. Conversely, show that any object isomorphic to a product object $A \times B$ is a product of A and B.

If a category $\mathbf{C}$ has a product $A \times B$ for every pair of objects A and B, we say that $\mathbf{C}$ **has all (binary) products**, or simply $\mathbf{C}$ **has products**.

It is often convenient to choose a particular product object $A \times B$ for each pair of objects A and B in a category $\mathbf{C}$ and refer to it as "*the product of A and B*." In this case, we say that $A \times B$ is the **distinguished product** of A and B, and that $\mathbf{C}$ "has **distinguished** (or **specified** or **chosen**) **products**."

Although it is customary to refer to the object $A \times B$ alone as a product object, it is important to remember that the projection arrows are also part of the definition. Strictly speaking, we should define the product as the tuple $(A \times B, \pi_1, \pi_2)$. This will become clearer in Section 1.9, where products are shown to be an instance of a more general construction called limits.

We can define arrows *between* product objects in terms of projection arrows:

1.5.3 Definition   If $A \times C$ and $B \times D$ are product objects, then for every pair of arrows $f : A \to B$ and $g : C \to D$, the **product map** $f \times g : A \times C \to B \times D$ is the arrow $\langle f \circ \pi_1, g \circ \pi_2 \rangle$.

Because category theory is such a strongly typed formalism, we can use symbols like π_1 and π_2 with no danger of confusion even though there are two different product objects being discussed here.

The dual notion, coproduct, corresponds to set-theoretic disjoint union:

1.5.4 Definition   A **coproduct** of two objects A and B is an object $A + B$, together with two injection arrows $\iota_1 : A \to A + B$ and $\iota_2 : B \to A + B$, such that for any object C and pair of arrows $f : A \to C$ and $g : B \to C$ there is exactly one arrow $[f, g] : A + B \to C$ making the following diagram commute:

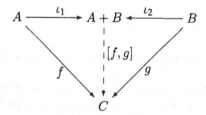

As with set-theoretic cartesian products and disjoint unions, the categorical constructions can be generalized to arbitrary indexed products and coproducts:

1.5.5 Definition   A **product** of a family $(A_i)_{i \in I}$ of objects indexed by a set I consists of an object $\prod_{i \in I} A_i$ and a family of projection arrows $(\pi_i : (\prod_{i \in I} A_i) \to A_i)_{i \in I}$ such that for each object C and family of arrows $(f_i : C \to A_i)_{i \in I}$ there is a unique arrow $\langle f_i \rangle_{i \in I} : C \to (\prod_{i \in I} A_i)$ such that the following diagram commutes for all $i \in I$:

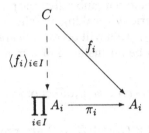

1.5.6 Exercises

1. Show that $\langle f \circ h, g \circ h \rangle = \langle f, g \rangle \circ h$. (Begin by drawing a diagram.)
2. Show that $(f \times h) \circ \langle g, k \rangle = \langle f \circ g, h \circ k \rangle$.
3. Show that $(f \times h) \circ (g \times k) = (f \circ g) \times (h \circ k)$.
4. Let X and Y be objects in a poset P considered as a category. What is a product of X and Y?
5. Let P and Q be objects in the category **Poset**. What is a coproduct of P and Q?
6. Name a category where some pair of objects lacks a product.
7. To what does Definition 1.5.5 reduce when the index set I is empty?

1.6   Universal Constructions

With some examples now in hand, we can give a general characterization of universal constructions.

A **universal construction** describes a class of objects and accompanying arrows that share a common property and picks out the objects that are terminal when this class is considered as a category.

For example, the definition of products of A and B in **C** describes a class of tuples (X, x_1, x_2), where $x_1 : X \to A$ and $x_2 : X \to B$:

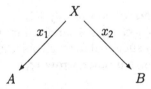

We might call these tuples "wedges over A and B," the objects of a "category of wedges over A and B." An arrow in this category, say

$m : (W, w_1, w_2) \to (X, x_1, x_2)$, is a **C**-arrow $m : W \to X$ such that $w_1 = x_1 \circ m$ and $w_2 = x_2 \circ m$:

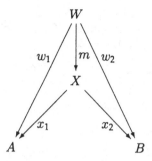

A terminal object in the category of wedges, say (P, p_1, p_2), is one with a *unique* arrow to it from each wedge:

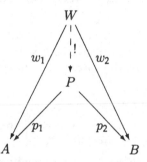

The object P is usually written $A \times B$; the arrows p_1 and p_2 are written π_1 and π_2. The unique arrow from a wedge (W, w_1, w_2) to $(A \times B, \pi_1, \pi_2)$, whose existence is guaranteed by the fact that $(A \times B, \pi_1, \pi_2)$ is terminal, is written $\langle w_1, w_2 \rangle$.

The entities defined by a universal construction are said to be **universal** among entities satisfying the given property, or simply to have the **universal property**. The unique arrows to them from other objects sharing the given property are often called **mediating arrows**.

A **co-universal construction** has the same form as a universal construction, except that the arrows are reversed and it picks out the *initial* object with the specified property.

1.7 Equalizers

Another basic universal construction is the equalizer of two arrows:

1.7.1 Definition An arrow $e : X \to A$ is an **equalizer** of a pair of arrows $f : A \to B$ and $g : A \to B$ if

1. $f \circ e = g \circ e$;
2. whenever $e' : X' \to A$ satisfies $f \circ e' = g \circ e'$, there is a unique arrow $k : X' \to X$ such that $e \circ k = e'$:

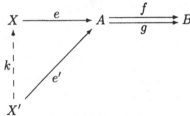

1.7.2 Exercise   Check that the elements of this definition correspond to the general description of universal constructions in the previous section.

1.7.3 Example   The category **Set** again provides an intuitive illustration. Let f and g be two functions in **Set** with common domain A and codomain B and let X be the subset of A on which f and g are equal, that is:

$$X = \{x \mid x \in A \text{ and } f(x) = g(x)\}.$$

Then the inclusion function $e : X \to A$, which maps each element $x \in X$ to the same x considered as an element of A, is an equalizer of f and g.

The dual construction, **coequalizer**, provides a categorical analogue to the set-theoretic notion of an equivalence relation.

1.7.4 Exercises

1. Show that in a poset considered as a category, the only equalizers are the identity arrows.
2. Show that every equalizer is monic.
3. Show that every epic equalizer is an isomorphism.

1.8   Pullbacks

Another useful categorical construct is the pullback of two arrows.

1.8.1 Definition   A **pullback** of the pair of arrows $f : A \to C$ and $g : B \to C$ is an object P and a pair of arrows $g' : P \to A$ and $f' : P \to B$

such that $f \circ g' = g \circ f'$

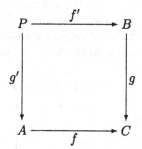

and if $i : X \to A$ and $j : X \to B$ are such that $f \circ i = g \circ j$

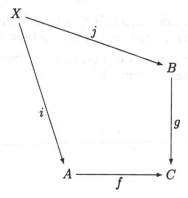

then there is a unique $k : X \to P$ such that $i = g' \circ k$ and $j = f' \circ k$:

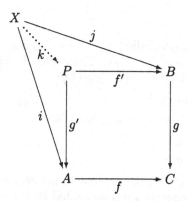

This situation is commonly described by saying that f' is a *pullback* (or *inverse image*) *of f along g* and that g' is a pullback of g along f. The example that motivates this terminology comes, as usual, from **Set**:

1.8.2 Example Let $f : B \to C$ be a function in **Set** and let $A \subseteq C$. Write $f^{-1}(A)$ for the set $\{b \mid f(b) \in A\}$, the inverse image of A under f, and $f|_S$ for the restriction of f to a set S (where $S \subseteq B$). Then the following diagram is a pullback—that is, it depicts a situation where the top and left sides of the square are the pullbacks of the bottom and right sides:

$$
\begin{array}{ccc}
f^{-1}(A) & \overset{\subseteq}{\longrightarrow} & B \\
{\scriptstyle f|_{f^{-1}(A)}}\big\downarrow & & \big\downarrow{\scriptstyle f} \\
A & \underset{\subseteq}{\longrightarrow} & C
\end{array}
$$

(To avoid a proliferation of symbols, $\subseteq$ is used as the name both of the inclusion function from A to C and of the one from $f^{-1}(A)$ to B.)

Saying that "the diagram is a pullback" is more rigorous than it sounds, as we shall see in Section 1.9.

1.8.3 Example If A and B are subsets of the set C, then

$$
\begin{array}{ccc}
A \cap B & \overset{\subseteq}{\longrightarrow} & B \\
{\scriptstyle \subseteq}\big\downarrow & & \big\downarrow{\scriptstyle \subseteq} \\
A & \underset{\subseteq}{\longrightarrow} & C
\end{array}
$$

is a pullback.

1.8.4 Example More generally, let $f : A \to C$ and $g : B \to C$ be two **Set**-arrows with common codomain C. The pullback object P is the subset of the cartesian product $A \times B$ defined by:

$$P = \{(a, b) \mid a \in A,\ b \in B,\ \text{and } f(a) = g(b)\}.$$

The projections f' and g' are defined by

$$
\begin{aligned}
f'(a, b) &= b, \\
g'(a, b) &= a.
\end{aligned}
$$

It is often helpful to think of pullbacks in general as *constrained products*, where the constraints are represented by the equation specifying that the first diagram in Definition 1.8.1 commutes.

The next two examples illustrate the interdefinability of many categorical constructs:

1.8.5 Example In any category with a terminal object, if

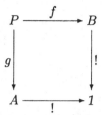

is a pullback, then P is a product of A and B. The arrows f and g are its projection functions.

1.8.6 Example In any category, if

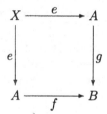

is a pullback, then e is an equalizer of f and g.

1.8.7 Exercises

1. (Pullback Lemma) Consider the following diagram:

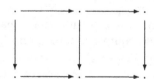

(a) Prove that if both of the squares are pullbacks, then the outside rectangle (with top and bottom edges the evident composites) is a pullback.

(b) Prove that if the outside rectangle and the right-hand square are pullbacks and the whole diagram commutes, then the left-hand square is a pullback.

2. Show that if

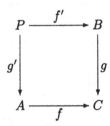

is a pullback and g is a monomorphism, then g' is also a monomorphism.

3. Show how to construct pullbacks from products and equalizers; that is, show that in any category where every two objects have a product and every two arrows have an equalizer, it is also the case that every two arrows with the same codomain have a pullback. (Hint: see Example 1.8.4.)

4. State the dual notion, **pushout**, and check that in **Set** the pushout of $f : A \to B$ and $g : A \to C$ is obtained by forming the disjoint union of $B + C$ and then identifying $\iota_1(f(x))$ with $\iota_2(g(x))$ for each $x \in A$ by a coequalizer.

1.9   Limits

Initial and terminal objects, products, co-products, equalizers, co-equalizers, pullbacks, and pushouts are examples of universal and co-universal constructions. These are all specific instances of the more general notions of limit and colimit of a diagram.

1.9.1 Definition Let **C** be a category and **D** a diagram in **C**. A **cone** for **D** is a **C**-object X and arrows $f_i : X \to D_i$ (one for each object D_i in **D**), such that for each arrow g in **D**, the diagram

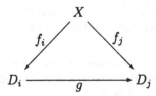

commutes. We use the notation $\{f_i : X \to D_i\}$ for cones.

1.9.2 Definition A **limit** for a diagram **D** is a cone $\{f_i : X \to D_i\}$ with the property that if $\{f_i' : X' \to D_i\}$ is another cone for **D** then there is a unique arrow $k : X' \to X$ such that the diagram

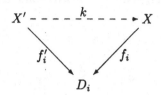

commutes for every D_i in **D**.

The cones for a diagram **D** form a category; a limit is a terminal object in this category. It follows that since terminal objects are unique up to isomorphism, so are limits.

1.9.3 Example   Given two **C**-objects A and B, let **D** be the diagram

$$A \qquad\qquad B$$

with two nodes labeled A and B and no edges. A cone for this diagram is an object X with two arrows f and g of the form:

$$A \xleftarrow{\;f\;} X \xrightarrow{\;g\;} B$$

A limiting **D**-cone, if it exists, is a product of A and B.

1.9.4 Example   Let **D** be the empty diagram with no nodes and no edges. A cone for **D** in a category **C** is any **C**-object. (**D** has no nodes so the cone has no arrows.) A limiting cone is then an object C with the additional requirement that for any **C**-object C' (i.e. for any **D**-cone) there is exactly one arrow from C' to C. In other words, C is a terminal object.

1.9.5 Example   Let **D** be the diagram

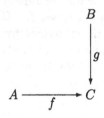

with three nodes and two edges. A cone for **D** is an object P and three
arrows f', g', and h such that the following diagram commutes:

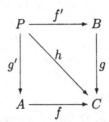

But this is equivalent to the commutativity of

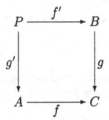

because h is completely determined as the common composite $f \circ g' = h = g \circ f'$.

If P, f', and g' form a limit, then they have the universal property
among objects and arrows that make this diagram commute—that is,
given any object P' with arrows f'', g'', and h' making the analogous
diagram commute, there will be a unique arrow k from P' to P such
that $f'' = f' \circ k$, $g'' = g' \circ k$, and $h' = h \circ k$. Ignoring h' again, this shows
that a limit of **D** is a pullback of f and g.

1.9.6 Definition Dually, a **cocone** for a diagram **D** in a category **C** is a
C-object X and a collection of arrows $f_i : D_i \to X$ such that $f_j \circ g = f_i$ for each g in **D**. A **colimit** or **inverse limit** for **D** is then a cocone
$\{f_i : D_i \to X\}$ with the co-universal property that for any other cocone
$\{f_i' : D_i \to X'\}$ there is a unique arrow $k : X \to X'$ such that the
diagram

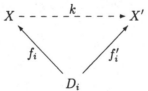

commutes for every object D_i in **D**.

Of course, not all diagrams have limits. For example, in a category with no terminal object, the empty diagram has no limit. In a category where the only arrows are identities—a **discrete category**—*no* diagrams with more than one node have limits. In fact, knowing which diagrams *do* have limits in a given category reveals a good deal about the category.

One pleasant possibility is that *all* limits exist in the category in question—that given any diagram **D**, there are always an object and arrows forming a cone for **D** and universal among such cones. In fact, a general theorem shows that if limits exist for very simple diagrams in a given category—products and equalizers—they must exist for arbitrary diagrams. (To be more precise, the theorem does not give the existence of all limits, but only limits of *small* diagrams—those whose sets of nodes and edges are really sets and not proper classes. See Remark 2.1.9.)

1.9.7 Theorem (Limit Theorem) Let **D** be a diagram in a category **C**, with sets V of vertices and E of edges. If every V-indexed and every E-indexed family of objects in **C** has a product and every pair of arrows in **C** has an equalizer, then **D** has a limit.

We first sketch the proof and then give it again in full detail. Both proofs can be skipped; nothing in the rest of the tutorial depends on them.

Proof Sketch: A good candidate for the limit object would be the product $\prod_{I \in V} D_I$ of the objects corresponding to the vertices of **D**, since this product comes equipped with an arrow to each D_I. But this won't quite work because the arrows from the product don't necessarily form commuting triangles with the edges D_e.

Form the product $\prod_{(I \xrightarrow{e} J) \in E} D_J$ of the targets of the edges of **D**. Now for each edge $D_e : D_I \to D_J$, there are two ways to get from $\prod_{I \in V} D_I$ to D_J: directly by π_J, or by $D_e \circ \pi_I$. Thus we can form two families of edges from $\prod_{I \in V} D_I$ to the D_J's. Since $\prod_{(I \xrightarrow{e} J) \in E} D_J$ is a product object, each family induces a mediating arrow from $\prod_{I \in V} D_I$ to $\prod_{(I \xrightarrow{e} J) \in E} D_J$. The refinement of $\prod_{I \in V} D_I$ that we need is one for which each arrow directly to D_J is equal to the one via D_e. This is the equalizer of the two mediating arrows.   (*End of Proof*)

1.9.8 Exercise Before reading the full proof, try to reproduce it from the proof sketch.

Proof: (Adapted from Arbib and Manes [1, p. 45]. Also see Mac Lane [67, p. 109].) Begin by forming the following V-indexed and E-indexed products and associated projections:

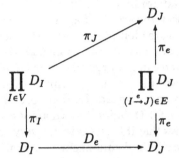

For each D_J at the top of the diagram there is an arrow π_J : $(\prod_{I \in V} D_I) \to D_J$. By the universal property of the product on the right, this implies the existence of a unique arrow p : $(\prod_{I \in V} D_I) \to (\prod_{(I \xrightarrow{e} J) \in E} D_J)$ such that $\pi_e \circ p = \pi_J$ for each edge $e : I \to J$. Similarly, for each D_J at the bottom right there is an arrow $(D_e \circ \pi_I)$: $(\prod_{I \in V} D_I) \to D_J$; this implies the existence of a unique arrow q : $(\prod_{I \in V} D_I) \to (\prod_{(I \xrightarrow{e} J) \in E} D_J)$ such that $\pi_e \circ q = D_e \circ \pi_I$ for each edge $e : I \to J$:

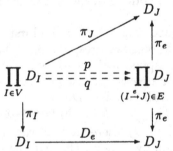

Let h be an equalizer of p and q. Set $f_I = \pi_I \circ h$ for each $I \in V$:

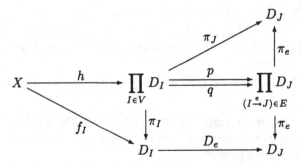

We claim that $\{f_I : X \to D_I\}$ is a limit for **D**. We must show first that it is a cone for **D**, and furthermore that it is universal among cones for **D**—that is, if $\{f_I' : X' \to D_I\}$ is also a cone for **D** then there exists a unique arrow $k : X' \to X$ with $f_I \circ k = f_I'$ for every vertex I.

Referring to the previous diagram, we can now establish the commutativity of the diagram

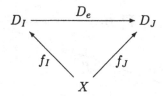

for each edge $e : I \to J$ in E:

$$
\begin{aligned}
D_e \circ f_I &= D_e \circ \pi_I \circ h && \text{(by the definition of } f_I) \\
&= \pi_e \circ q \circ h && \text{(commutativity of lower rectangle)} \\
&= \pi_e \circ p \circ h && \text{(since } h \text{ equalizes } p \text{ and } q) \\
&= \pi_J \circ h && \text{(commutativity of upper triangle)} \\
&= f_J && \text{(by the definition of } f_J).
\end{aligned}
$$

This shows that $\{f_I : X \to D_I\}$ is a cone for **D**. We must now show that it is universal among cones for **D**.

Assume that $\{f_I' : X' \to D_I\}$ is a cone for **D**. By the universal property of products, there is a unique arrow $h' : X' \to (\prod_{I \in V} D_I)$ such that $\pi_I \circ h' = f_I'$ for each $I \in V$. For any edge $e : I \to J$ in E,

$$
\begin{aligned}
\pi_e \circ p \circ h' &= \pi_J \circ h' && \text{(by the definition of } p) \\
&= f_J' && \text{(by the definition of } h') \\
&= D_e \circ f_I' && \text{(since } \{f_I' : X' \to D_I\} \text{ is a cone)} \\
&= D_e \circ \pi_I \circ h' && \text{(by the definition of } h') \\
&= \pi_e \circ q \circ h' && \text{(by the definition of } q).
\end{aligned}
$$

This establishes the commutativity of the diagram

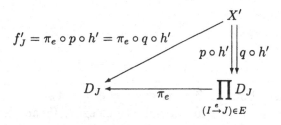

which, by the universal property of the product, implies that $p \circ h' = q \circ h'$—that is, h' equalizes p and q.

Since h is an equalizer of p and q, the universal property of equalizers guarantees the existence of a unique $k : X' \to X$ such that $h \circ k = h'$. It

is easy to see from the diagram

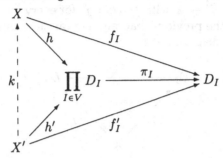

that

$$f_I \circ k = \pi_I \circ h \circ k = \pi_I \circ h' = f'_I.$$

Finally, we must show that k is the *only* arrow from X' to X such that $f_I \circ k = f'_I$ for all $I \in V$. But if any arrow k' satisfies $f_I \circ k' = f'_I$, then since $\pi_I \circ h \circ k' = \pi_I \circ h'$ for all $I \in V$, the universal property of the product guarantees that $h \circ k' = h'$ by the same argument as above. The unique arrow with this property is k, so $k = k'$.   (*End of Proof*)

1.9.9 Example One familiar application of the limit theorem is Scott's *inverse limit* construction, which gives a solution to the recursive equation $D \cong D \to D$ and forms the basis for a model of the lambda-calculus [102,103]. Intuitively, Scott's domain D_∞ is built by specifying an infinite chain of larger and larger domains, each embedded in the next with an arrow representing the embedding and an opposite arrow representing the corresponding projection, and then showing that there is a domain "at the limit." In categorical terms, the increasing domains are the objects and the embeddings and projections are the arrows of a diagram in an appropriate category; D_∞ is the colimit object of this diagram. Section 3.4 develops this example in more detail.

1.9.10 Exercises

1. Let **D** be the diagram

$$A \underset{g}{\overset{f}{\rightrightarrows}} B$$

Show that a limit for **D** is an equalizer of f and g.

2. In a poset $(P, \leq)$ considered as a category (Example 1.1.12), all diagrams commute. To what do the limit and colimit of a diagram correspond?

3. Specialize the proof of Theorem 1.9.7 to show how to construct limits of diagrams in **Set**. Show that essentially the same construction gives limits of diagrams in **Poset**.

4. Apply the dual of Theorem 1.9.7 to show how to construct colimits of diagrams in **Set**.

1.10   Exponentiation

Our last basic construction has special importance for theories of computation because it gives a categorical interpretation to the notion of *currying*, whereby a two-argument function is reduced to a one-argument function yielding a function from the second argument to the result.

We begin by sketching the construction in **Set**, then give the categorical definition. The presentation is adapted from Goldblatt's [40].

If A and B are sets, the collection

$$B^A = \{f : A \to B\}$$

of all functions with domain A and codomain B is itself a set. Similarly, in certain other categories **C** it is the case that $\mathbf{C}(A, B)$ is representable as an object B^A of **C**. (Part of what makes this observation interesting is that it does not hold in every category. It can be shown that there is no analogous construction in **Mon**, for example.)

As usual, we want to characterize B^A by arrows instead of elements. To do this, we observe that associated with B^A is a special *evaluation* function $eval : (B^A \times A) \to B$, defined by the rule $eval(f, a) = f(a)$. On input (f, a), with $f : A \to B$ and $a \in A$, it yields as output $f(a) \in B$.

The categorical characterization of B^A hinges on the observation that *eval* possesses a universal property among all functions $g : (C \times A) \to B$. For each such g, there is exactly one function $curry(g) : C \to B^A$ such that the following diagram commutes:

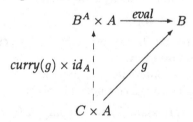

Recall that $curry(g) \times id_A$ denotes a product mapping (Definition 1.5.3). On input (c, a) it yields $(curry(g)(c), a)$.

Any particular $c \in C$ determines a function in B^A by fixing the first argument of g to be c, leaving the second argument free. Define g_c to be the *curried* version of g for a particular $c \in C$:

$$g_c(a) = g(c, a).$$

Then $curry(g)$ is just the function that takes each c to the appropriate curried version of g:

$$curry(g)(c) = g_c.$$

Now, for any $(c, a) \in C \times A$, we have:

$$\begin{aligned}
(eval \circ (curry(g) \times id_A))(c, a) &= eval(curry(g)(c), a) \\
&= eval(g_c, a) \\
&= g_c(a) \\
&= g(c, a).
\end{aligned}$$

This shows that the function $curry(g)$ makes the above diagram commute. To see that it is the only function that makes the diagram commute, note that $eval(curry(g)(c), a) = g(c, a)$ implies that $(curry(g)(c))(a) = g(c, a)$—that is, $curry(g)(c)$ must be a function that, for input a, yields $g(c, a)$. This function is g_c.

The general categorical definition is as follows:

1.10.1 Definition Let **C** be a category with all binary products and let A and B be objects of **C**. An object B^A is an **exponential object** if there is an arrow $eval_{AB} : (B^A \times A) \rightarrow B$ such that for any object C and arrow $g : (C \times A) \rightarrow B$ there is a unique arrow $curry(g) : C \rightarrow B^A$ making

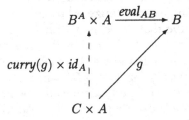

commute—that is, a unique $curry(g)$ such that

$$eval_{AB} \circ (curry(g) \times id_A) = g.$$

If **C** has an exponential B^A for every pair of objects A and B, then **C** is said to **have exponentiation.**

Categories with exponentials and products for all pairs of objects are important enough to deserve a special name:

1.10.2 Definition A **cartesian closed category** (CCC) is a category with a terminal object, binary products, and exponentiation.

1.10.3 Example The category **Set** is cartesian closed, with $B^A = \mathbf{Set}(A, B)$.

1.10.4 Example The category **CPO** of complete partial orders and continuous functions (Definition 3.4.6) is cartesian closed, with B^A the CPO of continuous functions from A to B.

1.10.5 Exercises

1. Give an example of a small finite category with products and a terminal object but without exponentials.

2. Exponentiation in **Set** × **Set** is "componentwise" the same as in **Set**. Check the details of the construction.

3. Give the construction of exponentiation in **Set**$^{\rightarrow}$. (Difficult. See Goldblatt [40, p. 88].)

4. Show that $curry(eval_{AB}) = id_{(B^A)}$.

5. Show that in any cartesian closed category, $B^{A \times A'}$ is isomorphic to $(B^A)^{A'}$.

6. The powerset operator $\mathcal{P}$ takes each set S to the set $\mathcal{P}(S) = \{T \mid T \subseteq S\}$ of all subsets of S. Given a set S, show that the partial order $(\mathcal{P}(S), \subseteq)$ is a cartesian closed category.

7. Let S be the set of sentences of propositional logic. We can consider S as a preorder $(S, \leq)$, where $p \leq q$ means that from p we can derive q. Show that S forms a cartesian closed category, where products are given by conjunction of propositions and the exponential q^p corresponds to "p implies q."

8. Explain how the category **FPL** of Example 1.1.15 can be extended with higher-order functions.

2 Functors, Natural Transformations, and Adjoints

> It should be observed that the whole concept of a category is essentially an auxiliary one; our basic concepts are essentially those of a functor and a natural transformation...
>
> — Eilenberg and Mac Lane [23]

2.1 Functors

In Section 1.1 we saw that many mathematical domains can be formulated as categories. Since categories themselves constitute a mathematical domain, it makes sense to ask whether there is a category of categories. In fact, there is: its objects are categories and its arrows are certain structure-preserving maps between categories, called functors.

2.1.1 Definition   Let **C** and **D** be categories. A **functor** $F : \mathbf{C} \to \mathbf{D}$ is a map taking each **C**-object A to a **D**-object $F(A)$ and each **C**-arrow $f : A \to B$ to a **D**-arrow $F(f) : F(A) \to F(B)$, such that for all **C**-objects A and composable **C**-arrows f and g

1. $F(id_A) = id_{F(A)}$
2. $F(g \circ f) = F(g) \circ F(f)$.

Type constructors provide a familiar example of functors from computer science:

2.1.2 Example   (Adapted from Rydeheard [96].) Given a set S, we can form the set $List(S)$ of finite lists with elements drawn from S. This defines a mapping $List$ that is the object part of a functor from **Set** to **Set**. The arrow part takes a function $f : S \to S'$ to a function $List(f) : List(S) \to List(S')$ that, given a list $L = [s_1, s_2, \ldots, s_n]$, maps f over the elements of L:

$$List(f)(L) = maplist(f)(L) = [f(s_1), f(s_2), \ldots, f(s_n)].$$

2.1.3 Example   The set $List(S)$ has some additional structure that we have not yet taken into account: an associative binary concatenation operation $*$ and an empty list $[\,]$ that acts as an identity for $*$, that is,

$[] * L = L = L * []$. Thus $(List(S), *, [])$ is a monoid (Example 1.1.6), and
$List : \mathbf{Set} \to \mathbf{Mon}$ is a functor taking each set S to the monoid of lists
with elements drawn from S.

The arrow part of $List$ takes a function f to a monoid homomorphism $List(f) = maplist(f)$. The fact that $maplist(f)$ is a homomorphism
corresponds exactly to the first two lines in a recursive definition of
$maplist$:

$$maplist(f)([]) = []$$
$$maplist(f)(L * L') = maplist(f)(L) * maplist(f)(L')$$
$$maplist(f)([s]) = [f(s)].$$

The third line ensures that these equations *define* the homomorphism
$maplist$, in the sense that it satisfies them uniquely. We shall have more
to say about this later.

$List(S)$ is often called the *free monoid generated by* S.

2.1.4 Exercise   Check that these equations are equivalent to the more
familiar definition of $maplist$:

$$maplist(f)([]) = []$$
$$maplist(f)([s] * L') = [f(s)] * maplist(f)(L').$$

One simple but very important class of functors is the forgetful functors, which operate by abstracting away from the structure of structured
objects. The letter U is often used to denote a forgetful functor because
it is sometimes thought of as extracting the "underlying" structure (typ-
ically a set) of an object:

2.1.5 Example   The **forgetful functor** $U : \mathbf{Mon} \to \mathbf{Set}$ sends each monoid
$(M, \cdot, e)$ to the set M and each monoid homomorphism $h : (M, \cdot, e) \to$
$(M', \cdot', e')$ to the corresponding function $h : M \to M'$ on the underlying
sets.

Another simple functor is the identity functor on a category:

2.1.6 Example   For each category $\mathbf{C}$, the **identity functor** $I_\mathbf{C}$ takes every
$\mathbf{C}$-object and every $\mathbf{C}$-arrow to itself.

The next class of functors will prove surprisingly useful later on:

2.1.7 Example   Let $\mathbf{C}$ be a category with a product $X \times Y$ for each
pair of objects X and Y. Then each $\mathbf{C}$-object A determines a functor
$(- \times A) : \mathbf{C} \to \mathbf{C}$, the **right product (with A) functor**, that takes each
object B to $B \times A$ and each arrow $f : B \to C$ to $f \times id_A$. (The "$-$" is used
to show where the argument object or arrow goes. A computer scientist
might write "$\lambda x. x \times A$" instead.)

The composition of two functors is given by separately composing their effects on objects and arrows. Given functors $F : \mathbf{A} \to \mathbf{B}$ and $G : \mathbf{B} \to \mathbf{C}$, the composite functor $G \circ F$ maps each $\mathbf{A}$-object A to the $\mathbf{C}$-object $G(F(A))$ and each $\mathbf{A}$-arrow $f : A \to A'$ to the $\mathbf{C}$-arrow $G(F(f)) : G(F(A)) \to G(F(A'))$. It is easy to check that this composition operation is associative and that the identity functors defined above are identities for composition of functors.

With this observation, we are ready to define the category of all categories:

2.1.8 Example The category **Cat** has categories as objects and functors as arrows.

2.1.9 Remark At this point, we should mention an important technical concern. The cardinality of **Cat** is clearly enormous, so that we might wonder whether it can consistently be considered as one of its own objects. (Readers familiar with Russell's Paradox in set theory may be concerned that there is a similar problem lurking in this definition. There is.) To avoid such questions, category theorists generally distinguish between **large** and **small** categories, where small categories are those whose collections of objects and arrows are both sets. Then **Cat** is defined more precisely to be the category of all small categories, which is itself a large category.

Readers interested in foundational issues should refer to a standard text on category theory such as Mac Lane [67] or Herrlich and Strecker [47]. Also relevant are papers by Mac Lane [66], Feferman [26], Grothendieck [42], Blass [8], Lawvere [63], and Benabou [6], and a chapter in Hatcher's book [46].

The functors we have considered so far have all been **covariant**. A **contravariant** functor is one that maps objects to objects as before, but that maps arrows to arrows going the opposite direction. This is not really a new concept, however, since a contravariant functor $F : \mathbf{C} \to \mathbf{D}$ is exactly the same as a covariant functor $F : \mathbf{C}^{\mathrm{op}} \to \mathbf{D}$. Similarly, product categories can be used to define n-ary functors. Two-argument functors are often called **bifunctors**.

2.1.10 Exercises

1. Check that the constructions in Examples 2.1.5 through 2.1.7 define functors.

2. Show that the powerset operator $\mathcal{P}$ can be extended to a functor $\mathcal{P} : \mathbf{Set} \to \mathbf{Set}$.

3. Let **M** and **N** be two monoids considered as one-object categories. What are the functors from **M** to **N**?

4. Let **C** be a category. The **diagonal functor** $\Delta : \mathbf{C} \to \mathbf{C} \times \mathbf{C}$ takes each **C**-object A to the object (A, A) in the product category $\mathbf{C} \times \mathbf{C}$. State the corresponding action of Δ on arrows and show that this defines a functor.

Our next example of functors plays an important role in category theory by allowing the sets of arrows between objects in an arbitrary category to be manipulated as *objects* in the category **Set** and capturing their behavior under composition as functions between these **Set**-objects.

2.1.11 Example   Given a category **C**, each **C**-object A determines a functor $\mathbf{C}(A, —) : \mathbf{C} \to \mathbf{Set}$. This functor takes each **C**-object B to the set $\mathbf{C}(A, B)$ of arrows from A to B and each **C**-arrow $f : B \to C$ to the function $\mathbf{C}(A, f) : \mathbf{C}(A, B) \to \mathbf{C}(A, C)$ defined by

$$\mathbf{C}(A, f)(g : A \to B) = f \circ g$$

where the composition on the right is in **C**. $\mathbf{C}(A, —)$ is called a **hom-functor**. (The origin of the term is in the frequent use of arrows in categories to model homomorphisms of various sorts. The set $\mathbf{C}(A, B)$ is often called a **hom-set**.)

Again, concern for consistency motivates a restriction: the collections of arrows between each two **C**-objects must be sets—not proper classes—for this definition to make sense. Categories with this property are said to be **locally small**.

2.1.12 Exercise   By analogy with Example 2.1.11, define a **contravariant hom-functor** $\mathbf{C}(—, B)$ and a bifunctor $\mathbf{C}(—, —)$ that is contravariant in its first argument and covariant in its second.

2.2 F-Algebras

Functors can be used to construct an elegant generalization of the category of Ω-algebras described in Example 1.1.7. (This section is needed only in Section 3.4 and may be skipped on a first reading.)

In Example 1.1.7 we defined a signature to be a set Ω of operator symbols equipped with a function $ar : \Omega \to \mathbb{N}$ specifying their arities. Given a signature Ω, an Ω-algebra A consists of a carrier $|A|$ and a collection of functions $\{a_\omega : |A|^{ar(\omega)} \to |A|\}_{\omega \in \Omega}$, one for each operator symbol ω.

Nothing essential is changed by saying that an Ω-algebra A consists of a carrier $|A|$ and a *single* function

$$a : \left(\sum_{\omega \in \Omega} |A|^{ar(\omega)} \right) \to |A|,$$

where $\sum$ is the set-theoretic disjoint-union operator, that is,

$$\sum_{\omega \in \Omega} |A|^{ar(\omega)} \;=\; \{ \; (\omega, (x_1, \ldots, x_{ar(\omega)})) \\ \mid \omega \in \Omega \text{ and } x_i \in |A| \text{ for all } 1 \le i \le ar(\omega) \},$$

and the function a maps an element $(\omega, (x_1, \ldots, x_{ar(\omega)}))$ of the disjoint union to $a_\omega(x_1, \ldots, x_{ar(\omega)})$.

The domain of a can be described as the image of $|A|$ under a functor $F : \mathbf{Set} \to \mathbf{Set}$, defined on objects by

$$F(S) \;=\; \sum_{\omega \in \Omega} S^{ar(\omega)}$$

and on arrows by

$$(F(g))(\omega, (x_1, \ldots, x_{ar(\omega)})) \;=\; (\omega, (g(x_1), \ldots, g(x_{ar(\omega)}))),$$

where $g : S \to S'$.

The functor F captures everything essential about Ω and ar, so we can think of F itself as a signature and define a notion of algebra with signature F, or *F-algebra*, consisting of a carrier set $|A|$ and a function $a : F(|A|) \to |A|$.

The notion of a homomorphism between Ω-algebras also has an analog for F-algebras. In Example 1.1.7, an Ω-homomorphism from A to B was defined to be a function $h : |A| \to |B|$ such that for each $\omega \in \Omega$ and $(x_1, \ldots, x_{ar(\omega)}) \in |A|^{ar(\omega)}$,

$$h(a_\omega(x_1, \ldots, x_{ar(\omega)})) \;=\; b_\omega(h(x_1), \ldots, h(x_{ar(\omega)})).$$

An F-homomorphism from $(|A|, a)$ to $(|B|, b)$ is a function $h : |A| \to |B|$ such that the following diagram commutes:

$$
\begin{array}{ccc}
F(|A|) & \xrightarrow{\;\;F(h)\;\;} & F(|B|) \\
{\scriptstyle a}\big\downarrow & & \big\downarrow{\scriptstyle b} \\
|A| & \xrightarrow[\;\;h\;\;]{} & |B|
\end{array}
$$

2.2.1 Exercise   Check that the two definitions of homomorphism are equivalent when F is defined from Ω as above.

We can now generalize the definition of F-algebra by replacing **Set** with an arbitrary category **K** and F by an arbitrary **endofunctor** on **K**—that is, an arbitrary functor from **K** to **K**:

2.2.2 Definition Let **K** be a category and $F : \mathbf{K} \to \mathbf{K}$ a functor. An F-algebra is a pair (A, a), where A is a **K**-object and $a : F(A) \to A$ is a **K**-arrow. An F-homomorphism $h : (A, a) \to (B, b)$ is a **K**-arrow $h : A \to B$ such that the following diagram commutes:

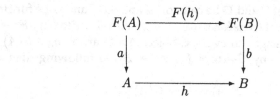

F-algebras are discussed in more detail by Arbib and Manes [1] (they use the term F-dynamic).

2.2.3 Remark   As presented here, this construction works only for algebras without equations (sometimes called *anarchic algebras*). The framework has apparently never been extended to include algebras with equations.

2.2.4 Exercises

1. Let **K** be a category and $F : \mathbf{K} \to \mathbf{K}$ an endofunctor on **K**. Check that F-algebras and F-homomorphisms form a category, **F-Alg**, with composition and identities inherited from **K**.

2. Show that if an F-algebra (A, a) is initial in the category **F-Alg** then a is an isomorphism.

Such an F-algebra is sometimes called a *fixed point* of F. Explain how this generalizes the usual notion of fixed points of a function f (values x for which $f(x) = x$).

2.3   Natural Transformations

Having defined mappings from one category to another—functors—we now proceed to define structure-preserving mappings, called natural transformations, from one *functor* to another. The concept of naturality is central in many of the applications of category theory; indeed, category theory itself was originally developed to deal systematically with natural transformations.

What is a structure-preserving map between functors? Given two functors $F : \mathbf{C} \to \mathbf{D}$ and $G : \mathbf{C} \to \mathbf{D}$, we can think of each of them as projecting a picture of **C** inside of **D**. Natural transformations arise when we imagine "sliding" the picture defined by F onto the picture defined by G. For each **C**-object A, we define an arrow η_A from the F-image to the G-image of A. To ensure that the structure of F is preserved by this transformation, we require that for each **C**-arrow $f : A \to B$ the transformations η_A and η_B take the endpoints of the F-image of f to the endpoints of the G-image of f.

2.3.1 Definition Let **C** and **D** be categories and let F and G be functors from **C** to **D**. A **natural transformation** η from F to G, written $\eta : F \xrightarrow{\cdot} G$, is a function that assigns to every **C**-object A a **D**-arrow $\eta_A : F(A) \to G(A)$ such that for any **C**-arrow $f : A \to B$ the following diagram commutes in **D**:

$$
\begin{array}{ccc}
F(A) & \xrightarrow{\eta_A} & G(A) \\
F(f) \downarrow & & \downarrow G(f) \\
F(B) & \xrightarrow{\eta_B} & G(B)
\end{array}
$$

If each component η_A of η is an isomorphism in **D** then η is called a **natural isomorphism**.

2.3.2 Example For any functor F, the components of the identity natural transformation $\iota_F : F \xrightarrow{\cdot} F$ are the identity arrows of the objects in the image of F, that is, $\iota_A = id_{F(A)}$. In fact, ι_F is a natural isomorphism.

Here is a particularly direct application of natural transformations in computer science:

2.3.3 Example Let *rev* be the function that reverses lists—that is, $rev_S : List(S) \to List(S)$ takes any list with elements in S to its reverse. For example,

$$rev_N [5, 6, 7] = [7, 6, 5].$$

This is an example of a *polymorphic* function—one that operates in exactly the same way, no matter what specific elements make up the list we provide as argument. If we substitute three other numbers, rev_N returns a new list with the substitutes in exactly the same configuration as before:

$$rev_N [6, 7, 8] = [8, 7, 6].$$

Indeed, we can apply any mapping whatsoever to the individual elements of the argument to *rev*, even one that changes their types. If $f : N \to S$, then

$$maplist(f)(rev_N [5, 6, 7]) = [f(7), f(6), f(5)].$$

In general, if $f : S \to T$ then

$$rev_T \circ maplist(f) = maplist(f) \circ rev_S.$$

This says precisely that *rev* is a natural transformation.

In categories with exponentiation, it turns out that the evaluation mapping forms a natural transformation. For simplicity, we give the construction in the category **Set**.

2.3.4 Example   For a fixed set A, the map taking B to $B^A \times A$ can be extended to a functor $F_A : \mathbf{Set} \to \mathbf{Set}$ as follows:

$$
\begin{aligned}
F_A(B) &= B^A \times A, \\
F_A(f : B \to C) &= (f \circ -) \times id_A.
\end{aligned}
$$

The fact that $eval : F_A \overset{\cdot}{\to} I_{\mathbf{Set}}$ is a natural transformation follows from the commutativity of the diagram

$$
\begin{array}{ccc}
F_A(C) = C^A \times A & \xrightarrow{\;eval_{AC}\;} & C = I_{\mathbf{Set}}(C) \\
{\scriptstyle F_A(g) = (g \circ -) \times id_A} \Big\downarrow & & \Big\downarrow {\scriptstyle g = I_{\mathbf{Set}}(g)} \\
F_A(B) = B^A \times A & \xrightarrow[\;eval_{AB}\;]{} & B = I_{\mathbf{Set}}(B)
\end{array}
$$

for each $g : C \to B$.

2.3.5 Example   Let **C** and **D** be categories. Let F, G, and H be functors from **C** to **D**. Let $\sigma : F \overset{\cdot}{\to} G$ and $\tau : G \overset{\cdot}{\to} H$ be natural transformations. Then for each **C**-arrow $f : A \to B$ we can draw the following composite diagram:

$$
\begin{array}{ccccc}
F(A) & \xrightarrow{\;\sigma_A\;} & G(A) & \xrightarrow{\;\tau_A\;} & H(A) \\
{\scriptstyle F(f)}\Big\downarrow & & {\scriptstyle G(f)}\Big\downarrow & & \Big\downarrow{\scriptstyle H(f)} \\
F(B) & \xrightarrow[\;\sigma_B\;]{} & G(B) & \xrightarrow[\;\tau_B\;]{} & H(B)
\end{array}
$$

Since both squares commute, so does the outer rectangle (by Proposition 1.2.4). This shows that the composite transform $(\tau \circ \sigma) : F \overset{\cdot}{\to} H$ defined by $(\tau \circ \sigma)_A = \tau_A \circ \sigma_A$ is natural.

Composition of natural transforms is associative and has, for each functor F, the identity ι_F. Thus, for every two categories **C** and **D**, we can form a **functor category** $\mathbf{D}^{\mathbf{C}}$, whose objects are the functors from **C** to **D** and whose arrows are natural transformations between such functors.

2.3.6 Example   The category **Cat** is cartesian closed, with $\mathbf{B}^{\mathbf{A}}$ the functor category.

2.3.7 Example   A category with no arrows other than identity arrows is essentially a set. If **C** and **D** are both sets then $\mathbf{D}^{\mathbf{C}}$ is also a set, namely the set of total functions from **C** into **D**.

2.3.8 Example   For any small category **C**, the functor category $\mathbf{C}^{\mathbf{1}}$ and **C** itself are isomorphic as objects of **Cat**. (**1** is the one-point category defined in Example 1.1.9.)

2.3.9 Example   Recall from Example 1.1.10 that **2** is a category with two objects and one non-identity arrow. For any category **C**, the functor category $\mathbf{C}^{\mathbf{2}}$ is isomorphic to the arrow category $\mathbf{C}^{\rightarrow}$ of Example 1.1.18. Its objects are arrows $f : A \rightarrow B$ of **C**. (Technically, they are functors from **2** to **C**, but each such functor picks out just one arrow in **C** and this choice completely determines the functor.) Its arrows are pairs (h, k) of **C**-arrows for which the following diagram commutes:

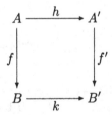

One reason that hom-functors (Example 2.1.11) are important is that they allow a large class of functors to be represented in a convenient elementary form:

2.3.10 Definition   Let **D** be a locally small category. A functor $F : \mathbf{D} \rightarrow$ **Set** is **representable** if there is a **D**-object R such that the hom-functor $\mathbf{D}(R, -)$ is naturally isomorphic to F. The object R is then called the **representing object.**

A longer discussion of representability is beyond the scope of this introduction, but it is often named as one of the two or three key concepts of category theory. The others, both closely related to representability, are adjoints (see Section 2.4) and universal elements (covered in any standard textbook).

2.3.11 Exercises

1. Check that the diagram in Example 2.3.4 commutes.

2. Let **P** be a preorder regarded as a category and let **C** be an arbitrary category. Let $S, T : \mathbf{C} \rightarrow \mathbf{P}$ be functors. Show that there is a unique natural transformation $\tau : S \xrightarrow{\cdot} T$ if and only if $S(C) \leq T(C)$ for every **C**-object C.

3. Show that the identity functor $I_{\mathbf{Set}} : \mathbf{Set} \to \mathbf{Set}$ is represented by any singleton set.

4. Show that the forgetful functor $U : \mathbf{Mon} \to \mathbf{Set}$ is represented by the monoid $(\mathbb{N}, +, 0)$.

5. (Open ended.) Extend the category $\mathbf{FPL}$ of Example 1.1.15 with lists and polymorphic functions on lists.

2.4 Adjoints

The slogan is, "Adjoint functors arise everywhere".

— Mac Lane [67]

The notion of adjoint, developed by Kan in 1958, is considered one of the most important ideas in category theory and perhaps the most significant contribution of category theory to the broader arena of mathematical thinking. A great variety of mathematical constructions—including many parts of category theory itself—are examples of adjoints.

Adjoints are more intricate than anything we have encountered so far. The best way to understand them is by working through the details of as many examples as possible. We begin with one important example, the free monoid, then give a formal definition of adjunction, and then proceed to further examples.

This section is inspired by Rydeheard's excellent short article [95].

We begin by showing that the free monoid $(List(S), *, [\,])$ of Example 2.1.2 has a very special property among monoids.

2.4.1 Proposition Let $f : S \to M$ be any function from a set S to the underlying set M of a monoid $(M, \cdot, e)$ and let i be the injection taking an element $s \in S$ to the singleton list $[s]$. Then there is exactly one monoid homomorphism

$$f^{\#} : (List(S), *, [\,]) \to (M, \cdot, e)$$

for which the following diagram commutes:

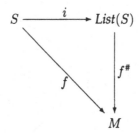

Proof: Define $f^\#$ to be the monoid homomorphism taking each list $[s_1, s_2, \ldots, s_n]$ to the product $f(s_1) \cdot f(s_2) \cdot \cdots \cdot f(s_n)$ in $(M, \cdot, e)$ and taking the empty list $[\,]$ to e. This definition clearly satisfies the conditions for being a monoid homomorphism (1 and 2) and makes the above diagram commute (3):

1. $f^\#([\,]) = e$
2. $f^\#([s_1, s_2, \ldots, s_n] * [t_1, t_2, \ldots, t_m])$
   $$= f^\#([s_1, s_2, \ldots, s_n]) \cdot f^\#([t_1, t_2, \ldots, t_m])$$
3. $f^\# \circ i = f$.

Now assume that some f' also satisfies these conditions. For any $L \in List(S)$, we show by induction on the length of L that $f'(L) = f^\#(L)$ and thus that $f' = f^\#$.

If $L = [\,]$, the first condition forces $f'(L) = e = f^\#(L)$. If $L = [s_1, s_2, \ldots, s_n]$ for some $n \geq 1$ then $L = [s_1] * [s_2, \ldots, s_n]$. By the third condition, $f'([s_1]) = f'(i(s_1)) = f(s_1) = f^\#(i(s_1)) = f^\#([s_1])$. By the induction hypothesis, $f'([s_2, \ldots, s_n]) = f^\#([s_2, \ldots, s_n])$. Now by the second condition, $f'(L) = f'([s_1]) \cdot f'([s_2, \ldots, s_n]) = f^\#([s_1]) \cdot f^\#([s_2, \ldots, s_n]) = f^\#(L)$.   (*End of Proof*)

The homomorphism $f^\#$ is called the *homomorphic extension of f* because it agrees with f on the elements of S, that is, $f^\#([s]) = [f(s)]$.

Let us make this construction more concrete by considering a particular instance.

2.4.2 Example The operation of the function *length* : $List(S) \to \mathsf{N}$ can be described by a set of recursive equations:

$$
\begin{aligned}
length([\,]) &= 0 \\
length(L * L') &= length(L) + length(L') \\
length(i(s)) &= 1.
\end{aligned}
$$

The first two lines of the definition are equivalent to the assertion that *length* is a homomorphism from the monoid $(List(S), *, [\,])$ of lists with elements in S to the monoid $(\mathsf{N}, +, 0)$ of natural numbers. The third line says that the following triangle commutes, where 1 is the constant function mapping every $s \in S$ to $1 \in \mathsf{N}$:

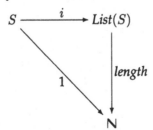

The properties of monoid homomorphisms together with the commutativity of the triangle correspond exactly to the definition of the *length* function. Thus, saying that the definition is proper—that it defines a function—is the same as asserting that there is a unique arrow making the triangle commute in the category **Mon**.

This brings us to the general definition of adjunction.

2.4.3 Definition   An **adjunction** consists of

- a pair of categories **C** and **D**
- a pair of functors $F : \mathbf{C} \to \mathbf{D}$ and $G : \mathbf{D} \to \mathbf{C}$
- a natural transformation $\eta : I_{\mathbf{C}} \overset{\cdot}{\to} (G \circ F)$;

such that for each **C**-object X and **C**-arrow $f : X \to G(Y)$, there is a unique **D**-arrow $f^{\#} : F(X) \to Y$ such that the following triangle commutes:

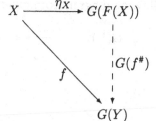

We say that (F, G) is an **adjoint pair** of functors; F is the **left adjoint** of G and G is the **right adjoint** of F. The natural transformation η is called the **unit** of the adjunction.

Let's check that this definition matches the example above. The categories **C** and **D** are **Set** and **Mon**, respectively. The functor F is *List* : **Set** $\to$ **Mon**. The functor G is the forgetful functor U : **Mon** $\to$ **Set**, which takes each monoid $(M, \cdot, e)$ to its underlying set M and each homomorphism to the corresponding function on the underlying sets. The natural transformation η is the family of functions $i_S : S \to List(S)$ that take each element of S to a singleton list. The $f^{\#}$ corresponding to the f that takes every element of S to the number 1 is the *length* function.

In the example the forgetful functor U was left implicit in several places—for example, wherever we considered a monoid homomorphism as a function on sets. Writing U everywhere it belongs, the diagram in the example matches the one in the definition precisely:

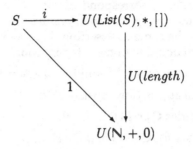

Associated with each adjunction is another natural transformation $\epsilon : (F \circ G) \to I_{\mathbf{D}}$, called the **co-unit** of the adjunction, with the property that for each **D**-arrow $g : F(X) \to Y$ there is a unique **C**-arrow $g^* : X \to G(Y)$ for which the following diagram commutes:

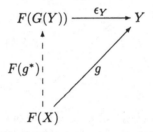

It can be shown that the existence of a unit implies the existence of a co-unit and vice versa. (See Barr and Wells [5] for a proof.) So we are free to choose whether to establish an adjunction by exhibiting the unit or the co-unit and whether to work with a given adjunction in terms of properties of the unit or the co-unit. It is not the case, however, that the unit and co-unit of an adjunction are dual constructions in the sense of Definition 1.1.16.

A given functor F may or may not have a right or left adjoint. The forgetful functor on a variety of algebras has a left adjoint, the *free algebra* functor, which takes a set S to the free algebra generated by the elements of S and a function $f : S \to S'$ to the homomorphic extension of f. The right adjoint, when it exists, usually describes a subset with some closure property. (See Cohn [17, p. 314].)

Adjoint functors have many useful properties. For example, functors that are left adjoints preserve colimits (i.e. map colimiting cones in the source category to colimiting cones in the target category) and, dually, right adjoints preserve limits.

There are other, equivalent definitions of adjunction. The one given above is probably the simplest for gaining an initial grasp of the concept; however, practicing category theorists normally prefer to think in terms of an isomorphism of hom-sets

$$\mathbf{D}(F(X), Y) \cong \mathbf{C}(X, G(Y))$$

that is natural in both X and Y—that is, a two-variable natural transformation between the hom-functors $\mathbf{D}(F(-), -)$ and $\mathbf{C}(-, G(-))$ that preserves structure as both arguments X and Y vary and that is a bijection for all X and Y. The bijection is often presented schematically:

$$\frac{X \to G(Y)}{F(X) \to Y}$$

Another way of saying the same thing is that adjointness occurs when there is an exact correspondence between $\mathbf{D}$-arrows from $F(X)$ to Y and $\mathbf{C}$-arrows from X to $G(Y)$:

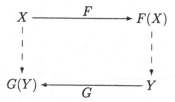

The reader who has persevered this far is urged to consult a standard textbook for more details on alternative treatments of adjoints. For the remainder of this section we will use the original definition and deepen the concept with several examples.

Categorical limits and colimits have a simple interpretation in terms of adjunctions, as the next three examples show.

2.4.4 Example   An initial object 0 in a category $\mathbf{C}$ arises as the image of the unique object of the category $\mathbf{1}$ under a left adjoint to the constant functor $T : \mathbf{C} \to \mathbf{1}$. The unit of the adjunction is the identity natural transformation $\iota : I_{\mathbf{1}} \dot{\to} I_{\mathbf{1}}$. The co-unit picks out the unique $\mathbf{C}$-arrow from 0 to each $\mathbf{C}$-object.

2.4.5 Exercise   Draw the unit and co-unit diagrams for this adjunction. In each diagram, what guarantees the existence of arrows from an initial object to every object of $\mathbf{C}$? What guarantees their uniqueness?

2.4.6 Example   If $\mathbf{C}$ is a category with a distinguished product object $A \times B$ for every pair of objects A and B, then the product functor $\Pi : \mathbf{C} \times \mathbf{C} \to \mathbf{C}$, which takes a pair of objects (A, B) to the object $A \times B$

and a pair of arrows (f, g) to the arrow $f \times g$, is a right adjoint of the diagonal functor $\Delta : \mathbf{C} \to \mathbf{C} \times \mathbf{C}$ of Exercise 2.1.10.4:

$$\frac{C \to A \times B}{(C, C) \to (A, B)}$$

The correspondence with Definition 2.4.3 is as follows:

$$
\begin{array}{ccc}
F & \leftrightarrow & \Delta \\
G & \leftrightarrow & \Pi \\
X & \leftrightarrow & C \\
Y & \leftrightarrow & (A, B) \\
\eta_C & \leftrightarrow & \langle id_C, id_C \rangle.
\end{array}
$$

The diagram for the unit of the adjunction is:

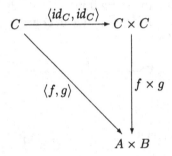

2.4.7 Exercise Draw the co-unit diagram for this adjunction. Prove that $A \times B$ satisfies the requirements of the definition of product (Definition 1.5.1).

2.4.8 Example In the definition of exponentiation (Definition 1.10.1), the assignment of a $curry(g)$ to each g establishes a bijection between the sets $\mathbf{C}(C \times A, B)$ and $\mathbf{C}(C, B^A)$. To see this, suppose $curry(g) = curry(h)$ for two functions $f, g : (C \times A) \to B$. Then $g = eval_{AB} \circ (curry(g) \times id_A) = eval_{AB} \circ (curry(h) \times id_A) = h$, so the assignment is injective. On the other hand, for any $g' : C \to B^A$, define $g = eval_{AB} \circ (g' \times id_A)$. By the uniqueness of $curry(g)$ it must be the case that $curry(g) = g'$, so the assignment is also surjective.

This correspondence of sets of arrows signals the presence of an adjunction:

$$\frac{C \to B^A}{C \times A \to B}$$

The details are as follows. First, pick a **C**-object A and hold it fixed during the construction. Now, the *right product* functor $(- \times A)$ of Example 2.1.7 has as its right adjoint the functor $(-)^A \times A$ of Example 2.3.4.

In this example the co-unit of the adjunction is more revealing than the unit. Here ϵ_Y is the evaluation arrow $eval_{AB}$ of Definition 1.10.1 and, for each $g : C \times A \to B$, the arrow $g^* : C \to B^A$ is $curry(g)$. Filling in the labels on the diagram that defines the co-unit, we see that it exactly matches Definition 1.10.1:

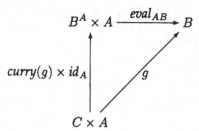

Finally, recall that the construction so far has assumed a fixed $\mathbf{C}$-object A. The category $\mathbf{C}$ has exponentiation if the functor $(- \times A)$ has a right adjoint for *every* A.

Many other mathematical constructions are examples of adjoints. Here are some briefer examples illustrating the range of situations where adjunctions can be found:

2.4.9 Example   Let $\mathbf{Int} = (\mathbf{Z}, \leq)$ and $\mathbf{Real} = (\mathbf{R}, \leq)$ be the integers and reals with the usual ordering, both considered as categories. It is easy to see that the inclusion $U : \mathbf{Int} \to \mathbf{Real}$ is a functor. In the other direction, the ceiling function $\lceil r \rceil$, which takes each $r \in \mathbf{R}$ to the smallest integer greater than or equal to r, is also a functor—that is, $r \leq r'$ implies that $\lceil r \rceil \leq \lceil r' \rceil$, where "$\leq$" in each case stands for an arrow. In fact, the ceiling functor is left adjoint to U. To see this, observe that $r \leq U(\lceil r \rceil)$ for each r. The collection of arrows representing this fact is the unit of the adjunction. The universal property of $U(\lceil r \rceil)$ in the diagram of Definition 2.4.3 corresponds to the word "smallest" in the definition of the ceiling function. (This example appears in Rydeheard and Burstall's book [98], where it is attributed to Pratt. Adjunctions between partial orders are also known as *Galois connections* [67,73].)

2.4.10 Example   (Also from Rydeheard and Burstall [98].) The category **Graph** has directed multi-graphs as its objects. An arrow $f : G \to H$ in **Graph** is a structure-preserving map between graphs—that is, a mapping v from vertices of G to the vertices of H and a mapping e from the edges of G to the edges of H, such that for each edge x of G, the endpoints in H of the image of x under e are the images under v of the endpoints of x in G. (Note the similarity to the definition of functors.)

Two nodes m and n in a graph G are said to be *strongly connected* if there is a path in G from m to n and a path from n to m. A subgraph $C \subseteq G$

is strongly connected if every pair of nodes in C is strongly connected. A strong component of a graph is a maximal strongly connected subgraph. The strong components of a graph themselves form an acyclic graph that is a quotient of the original graph—that is, each node corresponds to an equivalence class of strongly connected nodes in the original. The mapping taking a graph to the acyclic graph of its strongly connected components may be expressed as a left adjoint to the inclusion functor from **AcyclicGraph** to **Graph**.

2.4.11 Example   Goguen [31] defines a category of finite state automata and a category of observable behaviors. The *minimal realization* functor turns out to be left adjoint to the *behavior-of* functor. (Also see [36].)

2.4.12 Exercises

1. Dualize Example 2.4.4.

2. Show that the categorical coproduct (see Definition 1.5.4) arises as a left adjoint to the diagonal functor Δ.

3. What is the *unit* of the adjunction in Example 2.4.8? Give an intuitive interpretation to the mapping from f to $f^\#$.

4. Show that the floor function from **Real** to **Int**, which takes each real number r to the largest integer i such that $i \le r$, is right adjoint to the inclusion $U : \textbf{Int} \to \textbf{Real}$.

5. Show that the unit of an adjunction can be derived from the counit (and vice versa), and that the functors F and G determine each other to within a natural isomorphism.

3 Applications

This chapter uses the concepts developed in the tutorial to show some applications of category theory in computer science. Section 3.1 sketches the connection between cartesian closed categories and λ-calculus theories. Section 3.2 summarizes work by Reynolds on the design of programming languages using category theory. Section 3.3 surveys applications of category theory in the semantic description of programming languages. Section 3.4 describes in more detail the use of category theory as a unifying tool in domain theory.

3.1 Cartesian Closed Categories

One of the most widely cited connections between category theory and computer science is the correspondence between cartesian closed categories and typed λ-calculi. Space limitations make a full treatment here impractical; several of the references given in Chapter 4 give more details of the construction. Standard texts on λ-calculi are Hindley and Seldin [49] and Barendregt [3]; also see the tutorial articles by Cardelli and Wegner [15] and Mitchell [76].

A *typed λ-calculus* is an abstract programming language based on Church's simply typed λ-calculus [16]. Its types include a set K of base types, a product type $A \times B$ for each pair of types A and B, a terminal type *Unit*, and a functional type $A \to B$ for each pair of types A and B. Its expressions are given by the following abstract grammar:

$$M ::= unit \mid c \mid x \mid \lambda x{:}A.\, M \mid (M\ M) \mid (M, M) \mid fst\ M \mid snd\ M$$

The metavariable c ranges over a set C of constants, each with an associated type B_c; x ranges over variables. Expressions of the form $\lambda x{:}A.\, M$ are functional abstractions. Expressions of the form $(M\ M')$ are function applications. (M, M') is pairing; *fst* and *snd* are the corresponding projection functions. The variable x is said to be *free* in the expression x. The free variables of an expression $\lambda x{:}A.\, M$ are those of M, excluding x. The free variables of expressions of other forms are just the free variables of their subexpressions.

We write $\Gamma \vdash M : B$ to indicate that an expression M has type B when its free variables have the types declared in a context Γ. Formally, the valid typing assertions $\Gamma \vdash M : B$ are those that can be derived from the following set of *typing rules*:

$$\Gamma \vdash unit : Unit \qquad\qquad \textbf{(Unit)}$$

$$\Gamma \vdash c : B_c \qquad\qquad \textbf{(Const)}$$

$$\Gamma, x{:}A \vdash x : A \qquad\qquad \textbf{(Var1)}$$

$$\frac{\Gamma \vdash x' : A'}{\Gamma, x{:}A \vdash x' : A'} \qquad\qquad \textbf{(Var2)}$$

$$\frac{\Gamma, x{:}A \vdash M : B}{\Gamma \vdash \lambda x{:}A.\, M : A \to B} \qquad\qquad \textbf{(Abs)}$$

$$\frac{\Gamma \vdash M : C \to B \quad \Gamma \vdash M' : C}{\Gamma \vdash (M\ M') : B} \qquad\qquad \textbf{(App)}$$

$$\frac{\Gamma \vdash M : B \quad \Gamma \vdash M' : B'}{\Gamma \vdash (M, M') : B \times B'} \qquad\qquad \textbf{(Pair)}$$

$$\frac{\Gamma \vdash M : B \times B'}{\Gamma \vdash fst\ M : B} \qquad\qquad \textbf{(Fst)}$$

$$\frac{\Gamma \vdash M : B \times B'}{\Gamma \vdash snd\ M : B'} \qquad\qquad \textbf{(Snd)}$$

In addition to these typing rules, a typed λ-calculus comes equipped with a collection of *equivalence rules* specifying that certain expressions of the language represent the same value. For example, the rule

$$(\beta) \qquad (\lambda x{:}A.\, M)\, N = [N/x]M \in B,$$

describes function application. Here B is the type of both expressions; $[N/x]M$ is the result of substituting N for free occurrences of x in M. The rule

$$(\eta) \qquad (\lambda x{:}A.\, Mx) = M \in A \to B \quad \text{provided } x \text{ not free in } M$$

corresponds to the assertion that every element of a functional type is equivalent to some functional abstraction. In the presence of the other rules (in particular, the so-called ξ rule), this implies an *extensionality principle*: if two functions give the same result for all inputs then they are identical. There are several additional rules describing the behavior of products, substitution of equals for equals, and so on.

A λ-*theory* is a typed λ-calculus extended with some additional equivalences between expressions. For example, if the set K of base types contains *Int* and *Bool* and the set C of constants contains *zero, succ, true, false,* and *iszero*, then additional rules relating these constants may be given:

(*iszero zero*) = *true* ∈ *Bool*
(*not false*) = *true* ∈ *Bool*,
etc.

Given a λ-theory L, we can construct a category **CCC**(L) whose objects are the types of L. Each arrow $f : A \to B$ in **CCC**(L) corresponds to a class of equivalent terms of type B with one free variable of type A. For example, if x is a variable of type *Bool* then the equivalence class $\{x, \lambda y{:}x, not(not\ x), \ldots\}$ is an arrow from *Bool* to *Bool*. Terms with several variables are arrows from product objects. The built-in equivalence rules β, η, etc. are then used to show that **CCC**(L) is cartesian closed. The main technical difficulty is showing how substitution in L is translated into composition in **CCC**(L).

In the other direction, from an arbitrary cartesian closed category **C** we can define a λ-theory $\lambda T(\mathbf{C})$, called the *internal language* of **C**. Here the main difficulty is proving a *functional completeness* result that is needed to justify the definition of $\lambda x{:}A.\ M$ as an arrow.

In fact, the two translations turn out to be inverses:

$$\mathbf{CCC}(\lambda T(\mathbf{C})) \cong \mathbf{C} \quad \text{and} \quad \lambda T(\mathbf{CCC}(L)) \cong L.$$

Both translations are given in full in several of the references [2,60,61, etc.].

The correspondence between CCCs and λ-theories gives a convenient *algebraic* treatment of typed λ-calculi, which forms the basis for many current approaches to the semantics of polymorphic type systems (e.g. [2,107]).

A functor $F : \mathbf{C} \to \mathbf{D}$, where **C** and **D** are CCCs, is called a **cartesian closed functor** if it **preserves** terminal objects, products, and exponentials—that is, if it maps terminal objects, products, and exponentials, respectively, in **C** to terminal objects, products, and exponentials in **D**. A **functorial semantics** for a λ-theory L is a cartesian closed functor from **CCC**(L) to some CCC, usually **Set**.

The remainder of this section sketches a special case of the constructions described above, showing how to *interpret* a pure λ-theory L (one with no equations between expressions other than those required by the built-in rules) in an arbitrary cartesian closed category **C**. This amounts to spelling out the mapping formed by composing the translation from

L to $\mathbf{CCC}(L)$ with a semantic functor from $\mathbf{CCC}(L)$ into $\mathbf{C}$.

First, choose a $\mathbf{C}$-object $A_{\mathbf{C}}$ for each type $A \in K$.

Now define an *interpretation function* $[\![-]\!]$ from the types of L to the objects of $\mathbf{C}$ and from typing derivations in L into arrows of $\mathbf{C}$. The fact that we interpret typing derivations rather than expressions is an important technical point. In the present setting typing derivations are in one-to-one correspondence with well-typed terms—that is, if $\Gamma \vdash M : B$ is a valid typing assertion then there is exactly one proof using the above rules with this assertion as its last line—but for other sorts of λ-calculi this need not be so.

On types, $[\![-]\!]$ is given by:

$$
\begin{aligned}
[\![A]\!] &= A_{\mathbf{C}} \quad (\text{when } A \in K)\\
[\![Unit]\!] &= 1\\
[\![A \times B]\!] &= [\![A]\!] \times [\![B]\!]\\
[\![A \to B]\!] &= [\![B]\!]^{[\![A]\!]}.
\end{aligned}
$$

Note that the form of this definition implies that $\mathbf{C}$ must have *distinguished* products, exponentials, and terminal object.

The mapping $[\![-]\!]$ is defined on contexts by:

$$
\begin{aligned}
[\![\emptyset]\!] &= 1\\
[\![\Gamma, x{:}A]\!] &= [\![\Gamma]\!] \times [\![A]\!].
\end{aligned}
$$

To define $[\![-]\!]$ on typing derivations, we choose an arrow $c : 1 \to B_c$ for each constant $c \in C$ of type B_c. Now, if $x_1{:}A_1, \ldots, x_n{:}A_n \vdash M : B$ can be derived from the typing rules above then $[\![x_1{:}A_1, \ldots, x_n{:}A_n \vdash M : B]\!]$ will be an arrow from $((A_1 \times A_2)\ldots) \times A_n$ to B. This arrow is defined by induction on a proof whose last line is $x_1{:}A_1, \ldots, x_n{:}A_n \vdash M : B$, as follows:

1. $[\![\Gamma \vdash unit : Unit]\!] = \; ! \; : \; [\![\Gamma]\!] \to [\![Unit]\!]$

2. $[\![\Gamma \vdash c : B_c]\!] = c \circ ! \; : \; [\![\Gamma]\!] \to [\![B_c]\!]$

3. $[\![\Gamma, x{:}A \vdash x : A]\!] = \pi_2 \; : \; ([\![\Gamma]\!] \times [\![A]\!]) \to [\![A]\!]$

4. $[\![\Gamma, x{:}A \vdash x' : A']\!]$
   $= [\![\Gamma \vdash x' : A']\!] \circ \pi_1 \; : \; ([\![\Gamma]\!] \times [\![A]\!]) \to [\![A']\!] \quad \text{when } x' \neq x$

5. $[\![\Gamma \vdash \lambda x{:}A.\, M : A \to B]\!]$
   $= curry([\![\Gamma, x{:}A \vdash M : B]\!]) \; : \; [\![\Gamma]\!] \to ([\![B]\!]^{[\![A]\!]})$

6. $[\![\Gamma \vdash (M\,M') : B]\!]$
   $= eval_{CB} \circ \langle [\![\Gamma \vdash M : C \to B]\!], [\![\Gamma \vdash M' : C]\!] \rangle \; : \; [\![\Gamma]\!] \to [\![B]\!]$

7. $[\![\Gamma \vdash (M, M') : B \times B']\!]$
   $= \langle [\![\Gamma \vdash M : B]\!], [\![\Gamma \vdash M' : B']\!] \rangle \; : \; [\![\Gamma]\!] \to [\![B \times B']\!]$

8. $[\![\Gamma \vdash \mathit{fst}\ M : B]\!] = \pi_1 \circ [\![\Gamma \vdash M : B \times B']\!] : [\![\Gamma]\!] \to [\![B]\!]$

9. $[\![\Gamma \vdash \mathit{snd}\ M : B']\!] = \pi_2 \circ [\![\Gamma \vdash M : B \times B']\!] : [\![\Gamma]\!] \to [\![B']\!]$.

The correspondence between CCCs and λ-calculi also leads to an implementation technique for functional programming languages, the *categorical abstract machine* [19], and can be exploited to characterize evaluation strategies for functional languages [27,28].

3.2   Implicit Conversions and Generic Operators

...Our intention is not to use any deep theorems of category theory, but merely to employ the basic concepts of this field as organizing principles. This might appear as a desire to be concise at the expense of being esoteric. But in designing a programming language, the central problem is to organize a variety of concepts in a way which exhibits uniformity and generality. Substantial leverage can be gained in attacking this problem if these concepts are defined concisely within a framework which has already proven its ability to impose uniformity and generality upon a wide variety of mathematics.

— Reynolds [87]

In his paper "Using Category Theory to Design Implicit Conversions and Generic Operators" [87], Reynolds applies category theory to a subtle problem in the design of programming languages.

Most languages support at least a limited notion of *generic operator*. For example, it would be unfortunate to have to distinguish two separate addition operators:

$+_{Int}$: $\mathit{Int} \times \mathit{Int} \to \mathit{Int}$
$+_{Real}$: $\mathit{Real} \times \mathit{Real} \to \mathit{Real}$.

Instead, the single operator $+$ is considered to have two different signatures

$+$: $\mathit{Int} \times \mathit{Int} \to \mathit{Int}$
$+$: $\mathit{Real} \times \mathit{Real} \to \mathit{Real}$,

and the compiler is given the job of deciding which of these is intended in a given situation.

Another convenience provided by many languages is the ability to write an integer in a context where a real is expected, relying on the compiler to insert an *implicit conversion* from type *Int* to type *Real*. For example, if x is a *Real* variable and i is an *Int* variable, we would write

$x := i$

instead of

$x := Int\text{-}to\text{-}Real(i).$

The designers of some languages (notably PL/I and Algol 68) have combined these two mechanisms, making it possible to write

$x := i + j$

instead of

$x := Int\text{-}to\text{-}Real(i) +_{Real} Int\text{-}to\text{-}Real(j)$

or

$x := Int\text{-}to\text{-}Real(i +_{Int} j).$

But a question immediately arises: which of these two expressions did we mean? Unfortunately the usual approach—trying to give a set of rules specifying exactly where implicit conversions will be inserted in expressions involving generic operators—has led to complex, confusing, and even inconsistent language definitions. Reynolds suggests an alternative approach based on the observation that mathematically speaking it *doesn't matter* which interpretation of $x := i + j$ is chosen by the compiler. He proposes, in fact, that this observation be a requirement for the proper design of the conversions and generic operators themselves: their specification should not be considered well-formed unless they can be inserted in any order by the compiler without affecting the meaning of any program.

The mathematical tools Reynolds develops to carry out this program are a generalization of Higgins's *algebras with schemes of operations* [48], which in turn can be thought of as a generalization of the conventional *many-sorted algebras* used by Goguen, Thatcher, Wagner, and Wright [39]. The roots of this approach to the semantics of programs go back to Burstall and Landin [12]. Reynolds calls the present formalism *category-sorted algebra*.

The essence of the approach lies in viewing the types of a given programming language as forming a partial order Ω, for example:

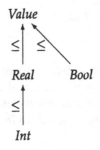

This partial order can be considered as a category, where the unique Ω-arrow $\sigma \leq \tau$ represents the fact that values of type σ may be implicitly converted to values of type τ. The conversion functions are the images of the $\leq$ arrows under a functor $B : \Omega \to$ **Set**. The object part of this functor maps each type σ to the set of values of type σ.

Finally, the fact that generic operators and implicit conversions may be inserted in either order by the compiler corresponds to the commutativity of diagrams like

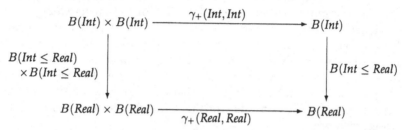

where γ_+ is a *family* of **Set**-functions for performing addition, indexed by the types of the two values being added.

Reynolds shows that such diagrams can be viewed as natural transformations. Moreover, these natural transformations have convenient descriptions in terms of adjunctions in many cases.

This view of data types leads to a general notion of algebraic semantics, which Reynolds uses in the second half of the paper to analyze a simple expression language derived from Algol 60. (Also see his paper on "The Essence of Algol" [88].) More recently, he has used similar techniques in designing the type system of the Forsythe language [90] and, with Oles, in describing the semantics of imperative languages with nested block structure [80,81]. The techniques of Reynolds and Oles are discussed in an introductory article by Tennent [115].

3.3   Programming Language Semantics

One area of computer science where the influence of category theory is particularly evident is semantic models of programming languages. Dybjer surveys the area in his article, "Category Theory and Programming Language Semantics: an Overview" [20]. This section summarizes the article; editorial comments appear in square brackets.

Dybjer distinguishes *mathematical semantics*, which concerns methods for interpreting programming languages in mathematical structures of set theory, algebra, or topology, from *operational semantics* [which concerns methods for directly describing the execution of programs]. The applicability of category theory to the latter seems to be minimal. Within mathematical semantics, Dybjer distinguishes topological methods (denotational semantics and domain theory) from algebraic methods (universal algebra). Both had early influence from category theory. In domain theory, Scott [102] showed that the continuous lattices with continuous functions form a cartesian closed category. In algebraic semantics, *algebraic theories* were developed by authors such as Elgot [24,25], Burstall and Thatcher [14], and the ADJ group [121]. [The idea of giving a categorical description of theories is originally due to Lawvere [62].]

Later, important papers by Wand [118] [also [119]], Smyth and Plotkin [110], and Lehmann and Smith [65] used category theory to unify different methods of solving domain equations and to connect denotational semantics with initial algebra semantics [see Section 3.4 of the present survey]. Barendregt [3, chapter 5] gives a natural unifying description of various models of the λ-calculus in terms of cartesian closed categories.

Dybjer goes on to discuss three specific approaches in more depth:

- The connection between category theory and *type theory* is based on Lambek's observation [58,59,60] [also [61]] that the cartesian closed categories are in perfect correspondence with a certain class of typed λ-calculi (the $\lambda\beta\eta$-calculi with surjective pairing). This has led a number of theorists to the conclusion that cartesian closure provides the appropriate notion of a model of the typed λ-calculus [104].

- The connection between category theory and *domain theory* is very rich, but complicated. Domain theory incorporates the notion of *partial elements* in order to assign meaning to programs whose execution may not terminate. This requirement has given rise to a number of formulations of domains as cartesian closed categories [7,43,85,86,102,105,106,109].

- The connection between category theory and *algebraic semantics* arises from the notion of *initial* or *free* algebra [12,25,37,121]. The abstract syntax of a programming language may be thought of as the initial object in a category of Σ-Algebras, where Σ corresponds to the grammar defining the language. [We used the term Ω-algebras for the same concept in Section 3.2.] A *meaning map* is the unique homomorphism from the initial algebra to some semantic algebra.

One controversial point in any discussion of the applicability of category theory to computer science is *how much* of category theory people are interested in using. Some authors [for example, Reynolds] use category theory simply as a powerful and uniform notational framework for masses of complicated but relatively elementary detail. On the other side, Dybjer cites papers by Lehmann [64] and Goguen and Burstall [35] where deep theorems of category theory are applied to computational situations.

3.4 Recursive Domain Equations

One of the great successes of category theory in computer science has been the development of a "unified theory" of the constructions underlying denotational semantics. Smyth and Plotkin's paper, "The Category-Theoretic Solution of Recursive Domain Equations" [110] builds on earlier work by Wand [119] to give a definitive category-theoretic treatment of this theory. This section develops a simplified version of their results.

Readers not familiar with domain theory may want to supplement this material with a textbook on denotational semantics. Schmidt [100] is excellent; Stoy [111] is also good.

In the untyped λ-calculus, any term may appear in the function position of an application. This means that a model D of the λ-calculus must have the property that given a term t whose interpretation is $d \in D$, there must be a way to regard d as an element of $[D \to D]$. Also, the interpretation of a functional abstraction like $\lambda x. x$ is most conveniently defined as a function from D to D, which must then be regarded as an element of D.

Let $\Psi : [D \to D] \to D$ be the function that picks out elements of D to represent elements of $[D \to D]$ and $\Phi : D \to [D \to D]$ be the function that maps elements of D to functions on D. Since $\Psi(f)$ is intended to *represent* the function f as an element of D, it makes sense to require that

$$\Phi(\Psi(f)) = f,$$

that is,

$$\Phi \circ \Psi = id_{[D \to D]}.$$

Furthermore, we often want to view every element of D as representing some function from D to D and require that elements representing the same function be equal—that is,

$$\Psi(\Phi(d)) = d$$

or

$$\Psi \circ \Phi = id_D.$$

The latter condition is called *extensionality*.

These conditions together imply that Φ and Ψ are inverses—that is, D is isomorphic to the space of functions from D to D that can be the interpretations of functional abstractions:

$$D \cong [D \to D].$$

Scott's inverse limit construction [102] provided the basic insight that if D ranges over a certain class of partially ordered sets and "$[D \to D]$" is taken to denote the mappings from D to D that are *continuous* on the ordering of D, then equations like this one can be shown to have nontrivial solutions. But there are many possible technical variations on the classes of domains and mappings for which the construction can be carried out. The details of the construction in each case are similar but not identical. To cope with a proliferation of special cases, Plotkin and Smyth (with Wand and others) developed a general characterization of the conditions under which a given equation has a solution in a given class of domains.

To make the example more interesting, let us suppose we are working with an untyped λ-calculus extended with a set C of built-in atomic constants. For the semantics of this calculus, we need a solution to the equation

$$D \cong A + [D \to D],$$

where A is some predetermined domain containing interpretations for elements of C. Each element of D corresponds to either an element of A or an element of $[D \to D]$, with a tag specifying which. This equation can be solved by finding least fixed points of the function

$$F(X) = A + [X \to X]$$

from domains to domains—that is, finding domains X such that

$$X \cong A + [X \to X],$$

and such that for any domain Y also satisfying this equation, there is an *embedding* of X into Y—a pair of maps

$$X \underset{f^R}{\overset{f}{\rightleftarrows}} Y$$

such that

$$f^R \circ f = id_X$$
$$f \circ f^R \sqsubseteq id_Y$$

where $f \sqsubseteq g$ means that f *approximates* g in some ordering representing their information content.

The key shift of perspective from the domain-theoretic to the more general category-theoretic approach lies in considering F not as a function on domains, but as a *functor* on a category of domains as described in Section 2.2. Instead of a least fixed point of the function F, we look for an *initial* fixed point of the functor F. We turn now to the task of developing enough of the general theory that we can state this precisely.

Recall from Section 2.2 that, given a functor $F : \mathbf{K} \to \mathbf{K}$, the category **F-Alg** has F-algebras as objects and F-homomorphisms as arrows. For present purposes, an alternative terminology is more suggestive:

3.4.1 Definition   Let $\mathbf{K}$ be a category and $F : \mathbf{K} \to \mathbf{K}$ a functor. A *fixed point* of F is a pair (A, a), where A is a **K**-object and $a : F(A) \to A$ is an isomorphism. A *prefixed point* of F is a pair (A, a), where A is a **K**-object and a is any arrow from $F(A)$ to A.

Prefixed points of F are F-algebras. The following is an immediate consequence of Exercise 2.2.4.2:

3.4.2 Fact   (Smyth and Plotkin's Lemma 1.) An initial F-algebra, if it exists, is also an initial fixed point of F in **K**—that is, it is initial in the category of fixed points of F, which is a subcategory of **F-Alg**.

The notion of initial fixed points provides a categorical way of talking about least solutions to sets of equations, when the equations are expressed as a functor F on a category **K**. Next we need some conditions on **K** and F that guarantee the existence of an initial F-algebra.

3.4.3 Definition   An ω-*chain* in a category **K** is a diagram of the following form:

$$\Delta = D_0 \xrightarrow{f_0} D_1 \xrightarrow{f_1} D_2 \xrightarrow{f_2} \cdots$$

Recall that a *cocone* μ of an ω-chain Δ is a **K**-object X and a collection of **K**-arrows $\{\mu_i : D_i \to X \mid i \geq 0\}$ such that $\mu_i = \mu_{i+1} \circ f_i$ for all $i \geq 0$. We sometimes write $\mu : \Delta \to X$ as a reminder of the arrangement of μ's components.

Similarly, a *colimit* $\mu : \Delta \to X$ is a cocone with the property that if $\nu : \Delta \to X'$ is also a cocone then there exists a unique mediating arrow $k : X \to X'$ (we will often say "from μ to ν") such that for all $i \geq 0$, $\nu_i = k \circ \mu_i$. Colimits of ω-chains are sometimes referred to as ω-*colimits*.

Dually, an ω^{op}-*chain* in **K** is a diagram of the following form:

$$\Delta = D_0 \xleftarrow{f_0} D_1 \xleftarrow{f_1} D_2 \xleftarrow{f_2} \cdots$$

A *cone* $\mu : X \to \Delta$ of an ω^{op}-chain Δ is a **K**-object X and a collection of **K**-arrows $\{\mu_i : X \to D_i \mid i \geq 0\}$ such that for all $i \geq 0$, $\mu_i = f_i \circ \mu_{i+1}$.

An ω^{op}-*limit* of an ω^{op}-chain Δ is a cone $\mu : X \to \Delta$ with the property that if $\nu : X' \to \Delta$ is also a cone, then there exists a unique mediating arrow $k : X' \to X$ such that for all $i \geq 0$, $\mu_i \circ k = \nu_i$.

We write $\perp_K$ (or just $\perp$) for the distinguished initial object of K, when it has one, and $!_{\perp \to A}$ for the unique arrow from $\perp$ to each K-object A. It is also convenient to write

$$\Delta^- = D_1 \xrightarrow{f_1} D_2 \xrightarrow{f_2} \cdots$$

to denote all of Δ except D_0 and f_0. By analogy, μ^- is $\{\mu_i \mid i \geq 1\}$. For the images of Δ and μ under F we write

$$F(\Delta) = F(D_0) \xrightarrow{F(f_0)} F(D_1) \xrightarrow{F(f_1)} F(D_2) \xrightarrow{F(f_2)} \cdots$$

and $F(\mu) = \{F(\mu_i) \mid i \geq 0\}$.

We write F^i for the i-fold iterated composition of F—that is, $F^0(f) = f$, $F^1(f) = F(f)$, $F^2(f) = F(F(f))$, etc.

With these definitions in hand, we can state Smyth and Plotkin's "Basic Lemma," which generalizes Tarski's theorem [113] that every monotonic function on a complete lattice has a least fixed point:

3.4.4 Lemma Let K be a category with initial object $\perp$ and let $F : K \to K$ be a functor. Define the ω-chain Δ by

$$\Delta = \perp \xrightarrow{!_{\perp \to F(\perp)}} F(\perp) \xrightarrow{F(!_{\perp \to F(\perp)})} F^2(\perp) \xrightarrow{F^2(!_{\perp \to F(\perp)})} \cdots$$

If both $\mu : \Delta \to D$ and $F(\mu) : F(\Delta) \to F(D)$ are colimits, then (D, d) is an initial F-algebra, where $d : F(D) \to D$ is the mediating arrow from $F(\mu)$ to the cocone μ^-.

Proof: Let (D', d') be any F-algebra. Define $\nu : \Delta \to D'$ by

$$\begin{aligned} \nu_0 &= !_{\perp \to D'} \\ \nu_{n+1} &= d' \circ F(\nu_n). \end{aligned}$$

First we show that ν is a cocone. We prove by induction that the following diagram commutes for all n:

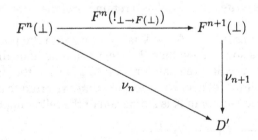

For $n = 0$ this is clear, since $\bot$ is initial. For $n + 1$ we have:

$$
\begin{aligned}
\nu_{n+2} \circ F^{n+1}(!_{\bot \to F(\bot)}) &= d' \circ F(\nu_{n+1}) \circ F^{n+1}(!_{\bot \to F(\bot)}) \\
&\quad \text{(by the definition of } \nu) \\
&= d' \circ F(\nu_{n+1} \circ F^{n}(!_{\bot \to F(\bot)})) \\
&\quad \text{(since } F \text{ is a functor)} \\
&= d' \circ F(\nu_n) \\
&\quad \text{(induction hypothesis)} \\
&= \nu_{n+1} \\
&\quad \text{(by definition).}
\end{aligned}
$$

To establish the theorem, we now need to show that there is a unique F-homomorphism $f : (D, d) \to (D', d')$.

First, suppose f is such a homomorphism. The uniqueness of f follows from the fact that it is the mediating arrow from μ to ν; to see this, we use induction again to show that $\nu_n = f \circ \mu_n$ for each n. Again, the case for $n = 0$ is clear. For $n + 1$, we have:

$$
\begin{aligned}
f \circ \mu_{n+1} &= f \circ d \circ F(\mu_n) &&\text{(by definition of } d) \\
&= d' \circ F(f) \circ F(\mu_n) &&(f \text{ is an } F\text{-homomorphism}) \\
&= d' \circ F(f \circ \mu_n) &&(F \text{ is a functor)} \\
&= d' \circ F(\nu_n) &&\text{(induction hypothesis)} \\
&= \nu_{n+1} &&\text{(by definition).}
\end{aligned}
$$

Second, to show that f exists, we *define* it as the mediating arrow from μ to ν (so that $\nu_n = f \circ \mu_n$ for all $n \geq 0$). We show that $f \circ d$ and $d' \circ F(f)$ are both mediating arrows from $F(\mu)$ to ν^-, which implies that they are equal and therefore that f is an F-homomorphism as required.

In the first case,

$$
\begin{aligned}
(f \circ d) \circ F(\mu_n) &= f \circ \mu_{n+1} &&\text{(by the definition of } d) \\
&= \nu_{n+1} &&\text{(by the definition of } f).
\end{aligned}
$$

In the second case,

$$
\begin{aligned}
(d' \circ F(f)) \circ F(\mu_n) &= d' \circ F(f \circ \mu_n) &&(F \text{ is a functor)} \\
&= d' \circ F(\nu_n) &&\text{(by the definition of } f) \\
&= \nu_{n+1} &&\text{(by the definition of } \nu).
\end{aligned}
$$

$$\text{(End of Proof)}$$

The Basic Lemma is a fundamental tool for finding initial fixed points of functors. But applying it directly in each situation where a fixed point is needed would be very tedious (see Exercise 3.4.20). To make it more useful, Smyth and Plotkin go on to develop the theory of O-categories, using a notion of embedding to capture the requirements for the applicability of the lemma to recursive domain equations. The remainder of this section summarizes a part of this theory, using the example from the beginning of the section as motivation.

To begin an attack on the problem of finding a solution to $X \cong A + [X \to X]$, we need to be more precise about the category in which we want the solution to live.

3.4.5 Definition   Recall that a partial order is a set P equipped with a reflexive, transitive, and antisymmetric relation $\sqsubseteq$. An *ω-sequence* is a sequence $\{p_i \mid i \geq 0\} \subseteq P$ in which $\forall i \geq 0$, $p_i \sqsubseteq p_{i+1}$. An *upper bound* of an ω-sequence $\{p_i \mid i \geq 0\}$ is an element p such that $\forall i \geq 0$, $p_i \sqsubseteq p$. The *least upper bound* (or *lub*) of $\{p_i \mid i \geq 0\}$ is an upper bound that is less than or equal to every other upper bound—that is, an element p such that p is an upper bound of $\{p_i \mid i \geq 0\}$ and, whenever p' is also an upper bound of $\{p_i \mid i \geq 0\}$, $p \sqsubseteq p'$.

A given ω-sequence may or may not have a lub. If an ω-sequence $\{p_i \mid i \geq 0\}$ does have a lub, it is written $\bigsqcup_{n \geq 0}^{P} p_n$ or just $\bigsqcup p_n$. A partial order in which every ω-sequence has a lub is called *ω-complete*. If it also has a least element (written $\bot_P$ or just $\bot$), it is called an *ω-complete pointed partial order*.

A function $f : P \to Q$, where P and Q are ω-complete pointed partial orders, is *monotonic* iff for all $p_1, p_2 \in P$, $p_1 \sqsubseteq p_2$ implies $f(p_1) \sqsubseteq f(p_2)$. It is *continuous* iff it is monotonic and for each ω-sequence $\{p_i \mid i \geq 0\}$ it is the case that $f(\bigsqcup_{n \geq 0}^{P} p_n) = \bigsqcup_{n \geq 0}^{Q} (f(p_n))$.

3.4.6 Definition   The category **CPO** has ω-complete pointed partial orders as objects and ω-continuous functions as arrows.

3.4.7 Exercise   Check that **CPO** satisfies the category laws of Definition 1.1.1.

CPO is *almost* a category where we can build solutions to equations like $X \cong A + [X \to X]$, but we need one further refinement: the notion of embeddings. (Incidentally, this is a good example of the common practice of studying categories whose hom-sets are **enriched** with extra structure.)

3.4.8 Definition   An **O-category K** is a category where

1. for every pair of **K**-objects A and B, the hom-set $\mathbf{K}(A, B)$ is equipped with an ω-complete partial ordering $\sqsubseteq_{\mathbf{K}(A,B)}$;

2. composition of **K**-arrows is an ω-continuous operation with respect to these orderings—that is, if $f \sqsubseteq_{\mathbf{K}(A,B)} f'$ and $g \sqsubseteq_{\mathbf{K}(B,C)} g'$, then $g \circ f \sqsubseteq_{\mathbf{K}(A,C)} g' \circ f'$, and if $\{f_i \mid i \geq 0\}$ is an ω-sequence in $\mathbf{K}(A, B)$ and $\{g_i \mid i \geq 0\}$ is an ω-sequence in $\mathbf{K}(B, C)$ then $\bigsqcup(g_n \circ f_n) = (\bigsqcup g_n) \circ (\bigsqcup f_n)$.

3.4.9 Exercise   Show that **CPO** is an **O**-category when its hom-sets are ordered *pointwise*:

$$f \sqsubseteq_{\text{CPO}(A,B)} f' \quad \text{iff} \quad \forall a \in A.\ f(a) \sqsubseteq_B f'(a).$$

3.4.10 Definition   Let **K** be an **O**-category and let $f : A \to B$ and $f^R : B \to A$ be **K**-arrows such that

$$f^R \circ f = id_A \quad \text{and} \quad f \circ f^R \sqsubseteq id_B.$$

Then f is called an *embedding* and f^R is called a *projection*.

3.4.11 Exercise   Show that each embedding f determines a unique projection f^R and vice versa.

3.4.12 Definition   If Δ is an ω-chain in an **O**-category **K**,

$$\Delta = D_0 \xrightarrow{f_0} D_1 \xrightarrow{f_1} D_2 \xrightarrow{f_2} \cdots$$

where each f_i is an embedding, then we write Δ^R for the ω^{op}-chain obtained by replacing each embedding f_i with the corresponding projection f_i^R:

$$\Delta^R = D_0 \xleftarrow{f_0^R} D_1 \xleftarrow{f_1^R} D_2 \xleftarrow{f_2^R} \cdots$$

3.4.13 Definition   Let **K** be an **O**-category. The *category of embeddings of* **K**, written $\mathbf{K}^E$, has as objects the objects of **K** and as arrows the **K**-arrows that are embeddings.

It is in $\mathbf{CPO}^E$ that we can construct initial fixed points of functors like $F(X) = A + [X \to X]$. In order to express F as a functor from $\mathbf{CPO}^E$ to $\mathbf{CPO}^E$, we need to define the more primitive functors A, $+$, and $[- \to -]$. Primarily because of the contravariance of $[- \to -]$ in its first argument, we must take a somewhat roundabout route. First, we define A, $+$, and $[- \to -]$ over **CPO** and $\mathbf{CPO}^{op}$ rather than $\mathbf{CPO}^E$. We use these to build a functor $G : \mathbf{CPO}^{op} \times \mathbf{CPO} \to \mathbf{CPO}$, from which we derive a functor $G^E : \mathbf{CPO}^E \times \mathbf{CPO}^E \to \mathbf{CPO}^E$. Finally, from G^E we derive the functor $F^E : \mathbf{CPO}^E \to \mathbf{CPO}^E$.

3.4.14 Definition   For any **CPO**-object A, the **constant functor** A is defined by:

$$A(B) = A,$$
$$A(f) = id_A.$$

3.4.15 Definition   The functor $+ : \mathbf{CPO} \times \mathbf{CPO} \to \mathbf{CPO}$ is defined on objects by

$$A + B = \quad \{(0, a) \mid a \in A\}$$
$$\cup \quad \{(1, b) \mid b \in B\}$$
$$\cup \quad \{\bot_{A+B}\},$$

where the partial order on $A + B$ is given by

$$
\begin{array}{ll}
c \sqsubseteq_{A+B} c' & \text{iff} \quad (c = \bot_{A+B}) \\
& \vee \quad (\exists a, a' \in A. \; c = (0, a) \; \wedge \; c' = (0, a') \; \wedge \; a \sqsubseteq_A a') \\
& \vee \quad (\exists b, b' \in B. \; c = (1, b) \; \wedge \; c' = (1, b') \; \wedge \; b \sqsubseteq_B b').
\end{array}
$$

The action of $+$ on arrows $f : A \to A'$ and $g : B \to B'$ is

$$
(f + g)(c) = \left\{
\begin{array}{ll}
(0, f(a)) & \text{if } \exists a \in A. \; c = (0, a) \\
(1, g(b)) & \text{if } \exists b \in B. \; c = (1, b) \\
\bot_{A'+B'} & \text{otherwise.}
\end{array}
\right.
$$

3.4.16 Exercise Show that $A + B$ is not necessarily a coproduct object in **CPO**.

3.4.17 Definition The functor $[- \to -] : \mathbf{CPO}^{\mathrm{op}} \times \mathbf{CPO} \to \mathbf{CPO}$ is defined on objects by

$$
[A \to B] = \mathbf{CPO}(A, B),
$$

the ω-complete pointed partial order whose elements are the continuous functions from A to B under the pointwise ordering:

$$
f \sqsubseteq_{[A \to B]} f' \quad \text{iff} \quad \forall a \in A. \; f(a) \sqsubseteq_B f'(a).
$$

The action of $[- \to -]$ on a $\mathbf{CPO}^{\mathrm{op}}$-arrow $f : A \to A'$ (that is, an ω-continuous function from A' to A) and a $\mathbf{CPO}$-arrow $g : B \to B'$ is:

$$
[f \to g](h) = g \circ h \circ f.
$$

We can't quite define F from these components. The expression $F(X) = A + [X \to X]$ does not define a functor on **CPO** at all because it uses its parameter on both sides of the $[- \to -]$ functor, which is contravariant in one argument and covariant in the other. On objects this is no problem. But when instantiated with an arrow $f : A \to B$ the expression becomes $A + [f \to f]$, which is poorly formed. We could perhaps save the situation by writing $F(f) = A + [op(f) \to f]$, where op is some function mapping arrows from A to B into arrows from B to A. But there is no such function: we cannot in general derive an ω-continuous function from B to A from an ω-continuous function from A to B.

However, using a similar idea we *can* define a functor $G : \mathbf{CPO}^{\mathrm{op}} \times \mathbf{CPO} \to \mathbf{CPO}$ that is only a small step away from F:

$$
\begin{array}{ll}
G(X, Y) & = \quad A + [X \to Y] \\
G(f, g) & = \quad A + [f \to g].
\end{array}
$$

The next step is to find a functor $G^E : \mathbf{CPO}^E \times \mathbf{CPO}^E \to \mathbf{CPO}^E$ that is covariant in both arguments.

3.4.18 Definition Let **K** be an **O**-category. A functor $T : \mathbf{K}^{\mathrm{op}} \times \mathbf{K} \to \mathbf{K}$ is *locally monotonic* iff it is monotonic on the hom-sets of **K**—that is, if for $f, f' : A \to B$ in **K**^{op} and $g, g' : C \to D$ in **K**, $f \sqsubseteq f'$ and $g \sqsubseteq g'$ imply that $T(f, g) \sqsubseteq T(f', g')$.

3.4.19 Fact   (Special case of Smyth and Plotkin's Lemma 4.) If $T :$ **K**$^{\mathrm{op}} \times$ **K** $\to$ **K** is locally monotonic, it can be used to define a covariant functor $T^E : \mathbf{K}^E \times \mathbf{K}^E \to \mathbf{K}^E$ by putting

$$
\begin{aligned}
T^E(X, Y) &= T(X, Y), \\
T^E(f, g) &= T(f^R, g).
\end{aligned}
$$

For our example, this functor is:

$$
\begin{aligned}
G^E(X, Y) &= A + [X \to Y], \\
G^E(f, g) &= I_A + [f^R \to g].
\end{aligned}
$$

Now, since G^E is covariant in both its arguments, we can define F^E simply by:

$$
\begin{aligned}
F^E(X) &= G^E(X, X), \\
F^E(f) &= G^E(f, f),
\end{aligned}
$$

or more explicitly:

$$
\begin{aligned}
F^E(X) &= A + [X \to X], \\
F^E(f) &= I_A + [f^R \to f].
\end{aligned}
$$

At this point we can check the conditions of Lemma 3.4.4 directly. The diagram Δ in **CPO**^{E} is:

$$
\Delta = \perp \xrightarrow{\;!_{\perp \to F^E(\perp)}\;} F^E(\perp) \xrightarrow{\;F^E(!_{\perp \to F^E(\perp)})\;} (F^E)^2(\perp) \cdots
$$

To be more succinct in what follows, we can abbreviate

$$
\begin{aligned}
\Delta_i &= (F^E)^i(\perp) \\
\delta_i &= (F^E)^i(!_{\perp \to F^E(\perp)}),
\end{aligned}
$$

and write:

$$
\Delta = \Delta_0 \xrightarrow{\;\delta_0\;} \Delta_1 \xrightarrow{\;\delta_1\;} \Delta_2 \xrightarrow{\;\delta_2\;} \cdots
$$

The colimit object D is (isomorphic to) the ω-complete pointed partial order whose elements are infinite tuples of *compatible* elements of the Δ_i's,

$$
D = \{\langle x_0, x_1, x_2, \ldots\rangle \mid \forall i \geq 0.\; x_i \in \Delta_i \;\wedge\; x_i = \delta_i^R(x_{i+1})\},
$$

with the *componentwise* ordering:

$$
\langle x_0, x_1, x_2, \ldots\rangle \sqsubseteq \langle x_0', x_1', x_2', \ldots\rangle \quad \text{iff} \quad \forall i \geq 0.\; x_i \sqsubseteq x_i'.
$$

The component arrows of the colimit $\mu : \Delta \to D$ are given by:

$$
\mu_i(x_i) = \langle \ldots, \delta_{i-2}^R(\delta_{i-1}^R(x_i)),\; \delta_{i-1}^R(x_i),\; x_i,\; \delta_i(x_i),\; \delta_{i+1}(\delta_i(x_i)),\; \ldots\rangle
$$

3.4.20 Exercise (Difficult and time-consuming!) The enterprising reader can gain a better appreciation for the importance of the more general theory to follow by working through the details of applying the basic lemma. The main steps are checking that:

1. D is an ω-complete pointed partial order;

2. μ is a colimit:

   (a) each μ_i is an embedding;

   (b) μ is a cocone;

   (c) if $\nu : \Delta \to D'$ is a cocone, then $k : D \to D'$, defined by $k = \bigsqcup(\nu_n \circ \mu_n^R)$, satisfies:

      i. k is an embedding;

      ii. $\forall i \geq 0.\ k \circ \mu_i = \nu_i$;

      iii. k is the unique arrow satisfying $\forall i \geq 0.\ k \circ \mu_i = \nu_i$;

3. $F(\mu) : F(\Delta) \to F(D)$ is a colimit.

Readers not familiar with the details of the domain-theoretic version of the inverse limit construction should consult a textbook for guidance. (Schmidt [100] is a good choice: he works with domains that are similar to these and provides about the right level of detail.)

We now summarize the steps in the more general approach. In brief, it consists of defining global conditions on a category $\mathbf{K}^E$ and a functor T^E that ensure the applicability of the basic lemma, and then finding easily checkable local conditions on $\mathbf{K}$ and T that imply the global conditions.

3.4.21 Definition A category $\mathbf{K}$ is an *ω-complete pointed category* (or just *ω-category*) iff it has an initial element and every ω-chain has a colimit.

3.4.22 Definition A functor $F : \mathbf{K} \to \mathbf{K}$ is *ω-continuous* iff it preserves ω-colimits—that is, if whenever Δ is an ω-chain and $\mu : \Delta \to A$ is a colimit, $F(\mu) : F(\Delta) \to F(A)$ is also a colimit.

3.4.23 Fact If $\mathbf{K}$ is an ω-category and $F : \mathbf{K} \to \mathbf{K}$ is ω-continuous, the conditions of the basic lemma are satisfied.

These are the global conditions. The local condition for a category $\mathbf{K}^E$ to be an ω-category is the existence in $\mathbf{K}$ of ω-limits. This is an instance of the well-known *limit/colimit coincidence* discovered by Scott [102].

3.4.24 Fact (See Smyth and Plotkin's Theorem 2.) Let $\mathbf{K}$ be an **O**-category and Δ be an ω-chain in $\mathbf{K}^E$. If Δ^R has a limit in $\mathbf{K}$, then Δ has a colimit in $\mathbf{K}^E$.

3.4.25 Fact **CPO** has all ω^{op}-limits.

Proof Sketch: Let Δ be the ω^{op}-chain:

$$\Delta = D_0 \xleftarrow{f_0} D_1 \xleftarrow{f_1} D_2 \xleftarrow{f_2} \cdots$$

Then the limit D (an ω-complete pointed partial order) is

$$D = \{\langle d_0, d_1, d_2, \ldots \rangle \mid \forall i \geq 0. \; d_i \in D_i \wedge d_i = f_i(d_{i+1})\}$$

under the componentwise ordering. The elements of the limit $\nu : D \to \Delta$ are the projections:

$$\nu_i(\langle d_0, d_1, d_2, \ldots \rangle) = d_i.$$

(End of Proof)

From these facts, it follows that $\mathbf{CPO}^E$ is an ω-category. All that remains is to show that F^E is ω-continuous.

3.4.26 Definition   Let $\mathbf{K}$ be an $\mathbf{O}$-category and $\mu : \Delta \to A$ a cocone in $\mathbf{K}^E$. Then μ is an $\mathbf{O}$-*colimit* of Δ provided that $\{\mu_n \circ \mu_n^R \mid n \geq 0\}$ is an ω-sequence in the ordering on $\mathbf{K}(A, A)$, and that $\bigsqcup(\mu_n \circ \mu_n^R) = id_A$.

The motivation for the definition of $\mathbf{O}$-colimits is purely technical: these are exactly the conditions that are needed to make Smyth and Plotkin's Theorem 2 go through. But they are not arbitrary: they will be familiar to anyone who has been carefully through the details of a domain-theoretic inverse limit construction.

3.4.27 Definition   An $\mathbf{O}$-category $\mathbf{K}$ is said to have *locally determined ω-colimits of embeddings* provided that whenever Δ is an ω-chain in $\mathbf{K}^E$, μ is a colimit of Δ in $\mathbf{K}^E$ iff μ is an $\mathbf{O}$-colimit of Δ.

3.4.28 Fact   (Corollary to Smyth and Plotkin's Theorem 2.) Suppose that $\mathbf{K}$ is an $\mathbf{O}$-category in which every ω^{op}-chain has a limit. Then $\mathbf{K}$ has locally determined ω-colimits of embeddings.

3.4.29 Definition   A functor $T : \mathbf{K}^{op} \times \mathbf{K} \to \mathbf{K}$ is said to be *locally continuous* iff it is continuous on the hom-sets of $\mathbf{K}$—that is, if whenever $\{f_n : A \to B \mid n \geq 0\}$ is an ω-sequence in $\mathbf{K}^{op}(A, B)$ and $\{g_n : C \to D \mid n \geq 0\}$ is an ω-sequence in $\mathbf{K}(C, D)$, then $T(\bigsqcup f_n, \bigsqcup g_n) = \bigsqcup(T(f_n, g_n))$.

3.4.30 Fact   (Smyth and Plotkin's Theorem 3.) If $T : \mathbf{K}^{op} \times \mathbf{K} \to \mathbf{K}$ is locally continuous and $\mathbf{K}$ has locally determined ω-colimits of embeddings, then T^E is ω-continuous.

Our functor G is easily shown to be locally continuous (from the definitions of the $+$, $[- \to -]$, and constant functors, and the fact that composition of functors preserves local continuity). Thus G^E is ω-continuous, from which it is easy to see that F^E is ω-continuous. By Fact 3.4.23, the conditions of the basic lemma are therefore satisfied by $\mathbf{CPO}^E$ and F^E. This gives us an initial F^E-algebra, which by Lemma 3.4.2 is also an initial fixed point of F^E in $\mathbf{CPO}^E$. Because the objects of $\mathbf{CPO}^E$ are the same as those of $\mathbf{CPO}$ and an isomorphism in $\mathbf{CPO}^E$ is also an isomorphism in $\mathbf{CPO}$, this gives us a solution in $\mathbf{CPO}$ to the equation $D \cong F^E(D)$.

4 Further Reading

This chapter lists and briefly describes the available textbooks, introductory articles, and general reference works on category theory. The last section gives a more eclectic sampling of research papers applying category theory in computer science.

4.1 Textbooks

Categories, Types, and Structures: An Introduction to Category Theory for the Working Computer Scientist (Asperti and Longo [2]) is a detailed treatise on category theory and its applications in denotational semantics. It includes an overview of category theory covering all of the standard topics and stressing connections with λ-calculus and recursion theory, as well as newer work by the authors and their colleagues on partial morphisms, internal category theory, and internal CCCs as models of the polymorphic λ-calculus.

Category Theory for Computing Science (Barr and Wells [5]) is an excellent new addition to the literature. Its coverage of aspects of category theory relevant to computer science is very broad, including several topics not covered in most introductions: the Grothendiek construction, the unifying notion of sketches ("a systematic way to turn finite descriptions into mathematical objects"), representable functors, cartesian closed categories, and **toposes** (categories with additional structure enabling certain set-like constructions; also known as **topoi**). Numerous exercises are given, with full solutions.

Topoi: The Categorial Analysis of Logic (Goldblatt [40]) is another excellent beginner's book. It is sometimes criticized by category theorists for being misleading on some aspects of the subject and for presenting long and difficult proofs where simpler ones are available. On the other hand, it makes liberal use of simple set-theoretic examples and motivating intuitions—much more than any other introduction. Although Goldblatt's main topic is topoi, the first 75 pages are devoted to standard category theoretic fundamentals and the later chapters on functors and adjoints can be read without the intervening material on topos theory. (Other standard works on topoi and categorical logic include books by Johnstone [54], Barr and Wells [4], and Lambek and Scott [61], and articles by Freyd [30] and Mac Lane [69].)

Computational Category Theory (Rydeheard and Burstall [98]) extends the authors' work on "programming up category theory," described in several earlier articles [11,13,97] and in greater depth in Rydeheard's thesis [94]. Starting from the observation that "categories themselves are the models of an essentially algebraic theory and nearly all the derived concepts are finitary and algorithmic in nature," it presents a self-contained introduction to roughly the same parts of category theory as the first two chapters of the present book, in almost entirely computational terms. Each concept is defined as a datatype in the ML programming language and each construction as an ML program.

Arrows, Structures, and Functors: The Categorical Imperative (Arbib and Manes [1]) was for several years the only usable introduction to category theory for nonmathematicians. Its treatment of the important basic concepts is fairly complete, and it provides a number of clear examples from areas of college algebra and automata theory that readers are likely to be familiar with. The exposition is extremely clear on most material, but somewhat less so in the most difficult sections.

Algebraic Approaches to Program Semantics (Manes and Arbib [72]) is a later book by the same authors. It presents a self-contained exposition of basic category theory and two different approaches to categorical denotational semantics—the *order semantics* of Scott and Strachey and the authors' own *partially additive semantics*. Except for mathematically mature readers, it may be too dense to be used as a first book on either category theory or semantics.

Categories (Blyth [9]) is a short introduction to basic category theory. The writing is terse and the examples are drawn solely from mathematics. The computer scientist whose purpose is to gain enough grounding in category theory to read research papers in computer science, as opposed to delving into category theory for its own sake, may find it hard work. However, it includes numerous exercises with solutions, making it a good choice for self-study if the reader has some background in algebra.

4.2   Introductory Articles

"A Junction Between Computer Science and Category Theory: I, Basic Definitions and Concepts (part 1)" (ADJ [36]) is the first of a well-known series of articles by the "ADJ group" at IBM (Goguen, Thatcher, Wagner, and Wright). It begins with a discussion of the relevance of category theory to computer science, introduces some background definitions and notation for sets and algebras, and develops the concepts of categories and functors. Copious examples are provided, mostly from algebra and automata theory.

"A Junction Between Computer Science and Category Theory: I, Basic Definitions and Concepts (part 2)" (ADJ [38]) continues the previous report. It covers graphs and diagrams and their relation to categories, as well as natural transformations. Again, the discussion is supplemented with numerous examples. One significant example—a categorical technique for proving correctness and termination of flow-diagram programs—is developed at length. The presentation of category theory in these two reports is incomplete, but pedagogically excellent: all definitions and examples are presented carefully and in good detail. (Two recent papers by Goguen [32,33] reiterate some of the same themes.)

"An Introduction to Categories, Algebraic Theories and Algebras" (Goguen, Thatcher, Wagner and Wright [37]) presents the ADJ group's categorical approach to universal algebra, based on Lawvere's concept of an algebraic theory [62]. It consists of a brief introduction to basic category theory, developed in parallel with exposition of algebraic theories and their applications to universal algebra.

"Notes on Algebraic Fundamentals for Theoretical Computer Science" (Thatcher, Wagner, and Wright [116]) is a broad summary of what, in the authors' view, is the necessary groundwork for mathematically sound work in theoretical computer science. In addition to a section on categories (which emphasizes adjoints), it contains material on set theory, partial orders, many-sorted algebras, ordered algebras, continuous algebras, algebraic theories, and the solution of equations within theories.

"Cartesian Closed Categories and Typed λ-Calculi" (Lambek [60]) is a fairly accessible introduction to the isomorphism between cartesian closed categories and typed λ-calculi, written by the developer of the idea. See Lambek and Scott's book [61] for a more complete development. (This idea is also discussed by Sander [99], Mitchell and Scott [77], and Barr and Wells [5]. Asperti and Longo's book [2] and a paper by Huet [50] give alternative formulations of the theory. Curien's categorical combinators [19] are also based on this connection.)

"Relating Theories of the λ-Calculus" (Scott [104]) gives a different development of the relation between cartesian closed categories and λ-calculi. The first section motivates CCCs as a general *theory of types*, from the perspective of the philosophy of logic. It then shows that theories in typed λ-calculus are cartesian closed categories. Later sections discuss the relation between typed and untyped λ-calculus, intuitionistic type theories and CCCs, and combinatory algebras. The early sections of the paper are fairly accessible.

"Some Fundamental Algebraic Tools for the Semantics of Computation: Part III: Indexed categories" (Tarlecki, Burstall, and Goguen [112]) is a short tutorial on the concept of **indexed category**, a way of handling "families of categories defined in a uniform way." Some examples of applications in computer science are given. (Another introduction to indexed categories appears in Taylor's thesis [114].)

"What Is Unification? A Categorical View of Substitution, Equation and Solution" (Goguen [34]) develops an elegant categorical view of the ubiquitous concepts of *substitution* and *unification*, applicable in a wide range of situations including type inference, logic programming, Scott domain equations, linear programming, and differential equations. The paper can also be used as a gentle introduction to basic category theory.

4.3   Reference Books

Categories for the Working Mathematician (Mac Lane [67]) is the standard reference on category theory. It cannot easily be used as an introduction to the subject, since it assumes considerable mathematical maturity and, especially for the examples, expertise in areas such as algebraic topology that the computer science reader almost certainly lacks. Nevertheless, Mac Lane's writing is sufficiently lucid that following along at 10% comprehension can be as valuable as checking every detail of another book. His volume belongs on the bookshelf of every serious student of the field.

Category Theory (Herrlich and Strecker [47]) is an excellent comprehensive reference on all aspects of pure category theory. Unlike most category theory texts, its level of pedagogical care is high enough and its prerequisites modest enough that it can profitably be read by any computer scientist who wants to understand a categorical concept in maximum depth and generality. It is currently out of print.

Abstract and Concrete Categories (Adamek, Herrlich, and Strecker [122]) is a new book with broad, up-to-date coverage and a similar attention to pedagogy. Its special emphasis is the theory of concrete categories.

Categories (Schubert [101]) is another good basic reference on pure category theory.

Abelian Categories (Freyd [29]) is a useful reference, particularly for the notion of representability.

Introduction to Higher Order Categorical Logic (Lambek and Scott [61]) aims at reconciling mathematical logic with category theory as approaches to the foundations of mathematics. The first section summarizes category theory from the perspective of categorical logic. The second section shows that typed λ-calculi are equivalent to cartesian closed categories and that untyped λ-calculi are similarly related to certain algebras. The third section explores the relationship between intuitionistic type theory and toposes. The final section discusses the representation of numerical functions (recursion theory) in various categories.

Categorical Combinators, Sequential Algorithms and Functional Programming (Curien [19]) develops a concrete approach to the semantics of sequential programming languages, motivated by the observation that computers manipulate not sets and functions but their concrete representations. A similar connection between cartesian closed categories and their equational descriptions leads to the notion of *categorical combinators*, which form the basis for the *Categorical Abstract Machine*, an implementation technique for functional programming languages.

Toposes, Triples and Theories (Barr and Wells [4]) develops three interconnected ideas. Toposes are special categories "defined by axioms saying roughly that certain constructions one can make with sets can be done in the category." Triples (also known as monads) capture much of the information in adjunctions and are useful in analyzing equational theories and properties of toposes. (Monads have also recently been used to give elegant accounts of some aspects of programming languages [79].) Categorical theories arise from an insight of Lawvere that "a mathematical theory—corresponding roughly to the definition of a class of mathematical objects—can be usefully regarded as a category of a certain kind, and a model of that theory—one of those objects—as a set-valued functor from that category which preserves the structure."

Algebraic Theories (Manes [71]) studies *equationally-definable classes* both set-theoretically and category-theoretically. For the computer scientist, it gives an abstract view of the mathematical structures from universal algebra and category theory that form the basis of many algebraic approaches to semantics. The book assumes some knowledge of algebra and topology but includes a self-contained presentation of "enough category theory for our needs and at least as much as every pure mathematician should know."

Algebra (Mac Lane and Birkhoff [68]) is a comprehensive undergraduate-level treatment of abstract algebra, organized according to the unifying "categorical insights" that have emerged in that field in the latter half of this century. Category theory *per se* is introduced at the end of the book, generalizing the special cases that have appeared throughout— for example, showing the step from concrete categories to arbitrary categories and from universal constructions to adjoints.

The Lambda Calculus (Barendregt [3]) is the standard reference on λ-calculus. It includes a discussion of models of the λ-calculus in cartesian closed categories.

Universal Theory of Automata: A Categorical Approach (Ehrig et al. [21]) presents a unified description of a theory of automata, encompassing deterministic, partial, linear, topological, nondeterministic, relational, and stochastic automata in a common categorical framework.

Theory of Categories (Mitchell [75]) was the first comprehensive exposition of category theory.

Universal Algebra (Gratzer [41]) is the standard reference on universal algebra, which has numerous applications in the study of semantics. Familiar structures studied in this field include lattices, free algebras, boolean algebras, and formal grammars. (Two other good books on universal algebra are Burris and Sankappanavar [10] and Cohn [17]. The latter is largely couched in categorical terminology.)

4.4   Selected Research Articles

"Type Algebras, Functor Categories, and Block Structure" (Oles [81]) presents a condensed version of results from the author's Ph.D. thesis [80]. It shows how category-theoretic notions, in particular functor categories, can be used to explain the semantics of languages with up-datable stores, procedures, and block-structure. In such languages, not only is the store itself modifiable but even the "shape" of the store can change as the program enters and exits blocks. Functors and categories of functors provide an elegant way of describing stores, semantics of expressions and programs, and algebras of types.

"Preliminary Design of the Programming Language Forsythe" (Reynolds [90]) describes the design of a language that aims at capturing the "essence" of Algol 60 [88] in as general and uniform a framework as possible. Category theory plays a central organizing role in the design and description of Forsythe's type system.

"Continuous Lattices" (Scott [102]) establishes the existence of semantic domains satisfying isomorphism equations like $D \cong D \to D$, thus providing the first known models of the untyped λ-calculus. Although this paper is couched in topological rather than categorical terms, the influence of categorical intuitions is apparent.

"Computational Lambda Calculus and Monads" (Moggi [79]) develops a general "categorical semantics of computation" based on monads, in which programs are interpreted as functions from values to *computations* rather than as functions from values to values. Different notions of computation can be defined to model partial functions, non-determinism, side effects, and continuations.

"A Category-Theoretic Account of Program Modules" (Moggi [78]) proposes a view of programming languages as indexed categories ([55, 112]) and illustrates this view with an application to the module system of the ML language [74]. Moggi's approach is superior to previous accounts of module systems because it accurately reflects the distinction between compile-time and run-time constructs. The paper also outlines a general methodology for analysis of programming languages, based on **2-categories** (categories with a category structure defined on their morphisms; see [56]).

"Declarative Continuations: an Investigation of Duality in Programming Language Semantics" (Filinski [27]) introduces a symmetric extension of the typed λ-calculus where continuations play a role dual to that of values, presents a type system for this calculus, and discusses various semantic issues. A categorical description of the language gives rise to a system of *symmetric combinatory logic*. The paper is a summary of results from Filinski's master's thesis [28].

"Categories of Models for Concurrency" (Winskel [120]) develops an abstract category-theoretic framework in which many concrete models of concurrent computation can be described and related.

"A Typed Lambda Calculus with Categorical Type Constructors" (Hagino [45]) develops the idea of using category theory as the basis for the type structure of a programming language, describes a uniform category-theoretic mechanism for declaring types, and presents a λ-calculus incorporating this mechanism. He shows that the evaluation of expressions in this calculus always terminates even though the calculus can be used to define infinite data structures. More details can be found in Hagino's Ph.D. thesis [44].

"On Functors Expressible in the Polymorphic Typed Lambda Calculus" (Reynolds and Plotkin [92]) develops a categorical proof of the nonexistence of a model of the polymorphic typed λ-calculus [91] in which types denote sets and $S \rightarrow S'$ denotes the set of all functions from S to S'. The paper is a joint exposition of Plotkin's generalization of an earlier result by Reynolds [89].

"Profinite Solutions for Recursive Domain Equations" (Gunter [43]) studies the category of *profinite* semantic domains, "an especially natural and, in a sense, *inevitable* class of spaces," and addresses some difficulties with solving recursive domain equations over the profinite semantic domains.

"Doctrines in Categorical Logic" (Kock and Reyes [57]) is a survey of category-theoretic methods in logic, organized by *doctrines*, that is, "categorical analogues of fragments of logical theories which have sufficient category-theoretic structure for their models to be described as functors." Equational, cartesian, finitary coherent, and infinitary coherent logic are covered, as well as (briefly) higher order logic and set theory.

"A Categorical Unification Algorithm" (Rydeheard and Burstall [97]) is an example of how categorical reasoning can be used to derive an algorithm. It is based on the observation that unification can be viewed as a coequalizer in an appropriate category. Adding some basic theorems about the construction of coequalizers provides a correctness proof of a recursive construction of the unification function. Finally, the construction is encoded in Standard ML. (The same derivation appears as a chapter in Rydeheard and Burstall's book [98].)

"Categories" (Pitt [82]) shows how functional programming languages can be thought of as categories. (This intuition has been extended to polymorphic functions by Rydeheard [96] and to higher-order functions by Wadler [117]. Hughes [52] uses the categorical formulation of polymorphism to develop a method of polymorphic strictness analysis for lazy functional programming languages.)

Bibliography

[1] Michael Arbib and Ernest Manes. *Arrows, Structures, and Functors: The Categorical Imperative*. Academic Press, 1975.

[2] Andrea Asperti and Giuseppe Longo. *Categories, Types, and Structures: An Introduction to Category Theory for the Working Computer Scientist*. The MIT Press, 1991.

[3] H. P. Barendregt. *The Lambda Calculus*. North Holland, revised edition, 1984.

[4] Michael Barr and Charles Wells. *Toposes, Triples, and Theories*. Springer-Verlag, 1984.

[5] Michael Barr and Charles Wells. *Category Theory for Computing Science*. Prentice Hall, 1990.

[6] Jean Benabou. Fibered categories and the foundations of naive category theory. *Journal of Symbolic Logic*, 50(1):10–37, March 1985.

[7] G. Berry and P.-L. Curien. Sequential algorithms on concrete data structures. *Theoretical Computer Science*, 20:265–321, 1982.

[8] A. Blass. The interaction between category theory and set theory. In J.W. Gray, editor, *Proceedings of the Special Session on the Mathematical Applications of Category Theory, 89th meeting of the American Mathematical Society*, number 30 in Contemporary Mathematics. American Mathematical Society, 1984.

[9] T. S. Blyth. *Categories*. Longman, 1986.

[10] Stanley Burris and H. P. Sankappanavar. *A Course in Universal Algebra*. Number 78 in Graduate Texts in Mathematics. Springer-Verlag, 1981.

[11] R. M. Burstall. Electronic category theory. In *Mathematical Foundations of Computer Science (Rydzyna, Poland)*, number 88 in Lecture Notes in Computer Science, pages 22–39. Springer-Verlag, 1980. Invited paper.

[12] R. M. Burstall and P. J. Landin. Programs and their proofs: an algebraic approach. *Machine Intelligence*, 4:17–43, 1969.

[13] R. Burstall and D. Rydeheard. Computing with categories. In Pitt et al. [83], pages 506–519.

[14] R. M. Burstall and J. W. Thatcher. An algebraic theory of recursive program schemes. In Manes [70], pages 126–131.

[15] Luca Cardelli and Peter Wegner. On understanding types, data abstraction, and polymorphism. *Computing Surveys*, 17(4), December 1985.

[16] Alonzo Church. A formulation of the simple theory of types. *Journal of Symbolic Logic*, 5:56–68, 1940.

[17] Paul M. Cohn. *Universal Algebra*. D. Reidel, revised edition, 1981. Originally published by Harper and Row, 1965.

[18] Guy Cousineau, Pierre-Louis Curien, and Bernard Robinet, editors. *Combinators and Functional Programming Languages*, number 242 in Lecture Notes in Computer Science. Springer-Verlag, May 1985.

[19] P.-L. Curien. *Categorical Combinators, Sequential Algorithms and Functional Programming*. Pitman, 1986. Available from John Wiley and Sons.

[20] Peter Dybjer. Category theory and programming language semantics: an overview. In Pitt et al. [83], pages 165–181.

[21] H. Ehrig, K.-D. Kiermeier, H.-J. Kreowski, and W. Kuhnel. *Universal Theory of Automata: A Categorical Approach*. B. G. Teubner, Stuttgart, 1974.

[22] S. Eilenberg and S. Mac Lane. Group extensions and homology. *Annals of Mathematics*, 43:757–831, 1942.

[23] S. Eilenberg and S. Mac Lane. General theory of natural equivalences. *Transactions of the American Mathematical Society*, 58:231–294, 1945.

[24] Calvin C. Elgot. Algebraic theories and program schemes. In E. Engeler, editor, *Symposium on Semantics of Algorithmic Languages*, number 188 in Lecture Notes in Mathematics, pages 71–88. Springer-Verlag, 1971.

[25] Calvin C. Elgot. Monadic computation and iterative algebraic theories. In Rose and Shepherdson [93], pages 175–230.

[26] Solomon Feferman. Set-theoretical foundations of category theory. In S. Mac Lane, editor, *Reports of the Midwest Category Seminar III*, number 106 in Lecture Notes in Mathematics, pages 201–247. Springer-Verlag, 1969.

[27] Andrzej Filinski. Declarative continuations: an investigation of duality in programming language semantics. In Pitt et al. [84], pages 224–249.

[28] Andrzej Filinski. Declarative continuations and categorical duality. Master's thesis, DIKU – Computer Science Department, University of Copenhagen, August 1989.

[29] Peter Freyd. *Abelian Categories: An Introduction to the Theory of Functors*. Harper and Row, 1964.

[30] Peter Freyd. Aspects of topoi. *Bulletin of the Australian Mathematical Society*, 7:1–76, 1972.

[31] J. A. Goguen. Realization is universal. *Mathematical Systems Theory*, 6(4):359–374, 1973.

[32] Joseph A. Goguen. A categorical manifesto. Technical Monograph PRG-72, Oxford University Computing Laboratory, Programming Research Group, March 1989.

[33] Joseph A. Goguen. Memories of ADJ. *Bulletin of the European Association for Theoretical Computer Science*, 36:96–102, October 1989. Guest column in the "Algebraic Specification Column".

[34] Joseph A. Goguen. What is unification? A categorical view of substitution, equation, and solution. In Maurice Nivat and Hassan Aït-Kaci, editors, *Resolution of Equations in Algebraic Structures*, volume I: Algebraic Techniques, chapter 6, pages 217–261. Academic Press, 1989. Also Technical Report SRI-CSL-88-2R2, Computer Science Lab, SRI International, January 1988, and Center for the Study of Language and Information, Stanford University, 1988.

[35] J. A. Goguen and R. M. Burstall. Some fundamental tools for the semantics of computation: Part 1: Comma categories, colimits, signatures and theories. *Theoretical Computer Science*, 31:175–209, 1984.

[36] J. A. Goguen, J. W. Thatcher, E. G. Wagner, and J. B. Wright. A junction between computer science and category theory: I, Basic definitions and concepts. Technical Report RC-4526, IBM Research, September 1973. (Part 1).

[37] J. A. Goguen, J. W. Thatcher, E. G. Wagner, and J. B. Wright. An introduction to categories, algebraic theories and algebras. Technical Report RC-5369, IBM Research, April 1975.

[38] J. A. Goguen, J. W. Thatcher, E. G. Wagner, and J. B. Wright. A junction between computer science and category theory: I, Basic definitions and concepts. Technical Report RC-5908, IBM Research, March 1976. (Part 2).

[39] J. A. Goguen, J. W. Thatcher, E. G. Wagner, and J. B. Wright. Initial algebra semantics and continuous algebras. *Journal of the ACM*, 24(1):68–95, 1977.

[40] Robert Goldblatt. *Topoi: The Categorial Analysis of Logic*. North Holland, 1984.

[41] George Gratzer. *Universal Algebra*. Van Nostrand, 1968.

[42] A. Grothendieck. Categories fibrees et descente. In *Revêtements Etales et Group Fondamental: Seminaire de Geometrie Algebrique du Bois Marie 1960/61 (SGA 1), Expose VI*. Institut des Hautes Etudes Scientifiques, Paris, 1963. Reprinted in Lecture Notes in Mathematics No. 224, Springer-Verlag, 1971.

[43] Carl Gunter. *Profinite Solutions for Recursive Domain Equations*. PhD thesis, University of Wisconson, 1985. Available as Carnegie Mellon University School of Computer Science Technical Report CMU-CS-85-107.

[44] Tatsuya Hagino. *A Category Theoretic Approach to Data Types*. PhD thesis, University of Edinburgh, Department of Computer Science, 1987. CST-47-87 (also published as ECS-LFCS-87-38).

[45] Tatsuya Hagino. A typed lambda calculus with categorical type constructors. In D. H. Pitt, A. Poigne, and D. E. Rydeheard, editors, *Category Theory and Computer Science (Edinburgh, U.K.)*, number 283 in Lecture Notes in Computer Science. Springer-Verlag, September 1987.

[46] William S. Hatcher. *Foundations of Mathematics*. W. B. Saunders Co., 1968.

[47] Horst Herrlich and George E. Strecker. *Category Theory*. Allyn and Bacon, 1973.

[48] P. J. Higgins. Algebras with a schema of operators. *Mathematische Nachrichten*, 27:115–132, 1963.

[49] J. Roger Hindley and Jonathan P. Seldin. *Introduction to Combinators and λ-Calculus*, volume 1 of *London Mathematical Society Student Texts*. Cambridge University Press, 1986.

[50] Gerard Huet. Cartesian closed categories and lambda calculus. In Cousineau et al. [18].

[51] Gerard Huet, editor. *Logical Foundations of Functional Programming*. University of Texas at Austin Year of Programming Series. Addison-Wesley, 1990.

[52] John Hughes. Projections for polymorphic strictness analysis. In Pitt et al. [84], pages 82–100.

[53] W. Hurewicz. On duality theorems. *Bulletin of the American Mathematical Society*, 47:562–563, 1941.

[54] P. T. Johnstone. *Topos Theory*. Academic Press, 1977.

[55] P. T. Johnstone and R. Pare, editors. *Indexed Categories and Their Applications*, number 661 in Lecture Notes in Mathematics. Springer-Verlag, 1978.

[56] G. M. Kelly and Ross Street. Review of the elements of 2-categories. In Gregory M. Kelly, editor, *Category Seminar: Proceedings Sydney Category Seminar 1972/1973*, number 420 in Lecture Notes in Mathematics. Springer-Verlag, 1974.

[57] A. Kock and G. E. Reyes. Doctrines in categorical logic. In J. Barwise, editor, *Handbook of Mathematical Logic*, pages 283–313. North Holland, 1977.

[58] Joachim Lambek. Deductive systems and categories: II: Standard constructions and closed categories. In *Category theory, homology theory and their applications*, number 86 in Lecture Notes in Mathematics, pages 76–122. Springer-Verlag, 1969.

[59] J. Lambek. From λ-calculus to cartesian closed categories. In Seldin and Hindley [108], pages 375–402.

[60] J. Lambek. Cartesian closed categories and typed lambda-calculi. In Cousineau et al. [18].

[61] J. Lambek and P. J. Scott. *Introduction to higher order categorical logic*. Number 7 in Cambridge Studies in Advanced Mathematics. Cambridge University Press, 1986. First paperback edition (with corrections) 1988.

[62] F. W. Lawvere. *Functorial Semantics of Algebraic Theories*. PhD thesis, Columbia University, 1963. Announcement in Proceedings of the National Academy of Science 50 (1963), pp. 869-873.

[63] F. William Lawvere. The category of categories as a foundation for mathematics. In S. Eilenberg, D.K. Harrison, S. Mac Lane, and H. Rohrl, editors, *Proceedings of the Conference on Categorical Algebra (La Jolla, 1965)*, pages 1–20. Springer-Verlag, 1966.

[64] Daniel J. Lehmann. On the algebra of order. *Journal of Computer and System Sciences*, 21:1–23, 1980.

[65] D. J. Lehmann and M. B. Smyth. Data types (extended abstract). In *Proceedings 18th IEEE Symposium on Foundations of Computer Science*, pages 7–12, 1977.

[66] Saunders Mac Lane. One universe as a foundation for category theory. In S. Mac Lane, editor, *Reports of the Midwest Category Seminar III*, number 106 in Lecture Notes in Mathematics, pages 192–200. Springer-Verlag, 1969.

[67] Saunders Mac Lane. *Categories for the Working Mathematician*. Springer-Verlag, 1971.

[68] Saunders Mac Lane and Garrett Birkhoff. *Algebra*. MacMillan, 1967.

[69] Saunders Maclane. Sets, topoi, and internal logic in categories. In Rose and Shepherdson [93], pages 119–134.

[70] E. G. Manes, editor. *Proceedings of the AAAS Symposium on Category Theory Applied to Computation and Control (San Francisco, California)*, number 25 in Lecture Notes in Computer Science. Springer-Verlag, 1975.

[71] Ernest G. Manes. *Algebraic Theories*. Number 26 in Graduate Texts in Mathematics. Springer-Verlag, 1976.

[72] Ernest Manes and Michael Arbib. *Algebraic Approaches to Program Semantics*. Springer-Verlag, 1986.

[73] A. Melton, D. A. Schmidt, and G. E. Strecker. Galois connections and computer science applications. In Pitt et al. [83], pages 299–312.

[74] Robin Milner, Mads Tofte, and Robert Harper. *The Definition of Standard ML*. The MIT Press, 1990.

[75] Barry Mitchell. *Theory of Categories*. Academic Press, 1965.

[76] John C. Mitchell. Type systems for programming languages. Technical Report STAN-CS-89-1277, Department of Computer Science, Stanford University, July 1989. To appear as a chapter in Handbook of Theoretical Computer Science, van Leeuwen et al., North-Holland.

[77] John C. Mitchell and Philip J. Scott. Typed lambda models and cartesian closed categories (preliminary version). In John W. Gray and Andre Scedrov, editors, *Categories in Computer Science and Logic (Boulder, Colorado)*, number 92 in Contemporary Mathematics, pages 301–316. American Mathematical Society, June 1987.

[78] Eugenio Moggi. A category-theoretic account of program modules. In Pitt et al. [84], pages 101–117.

[79] Eugenio Moggi. Computational lambda-calculus and monads. In *Fourth Annual Symposium on Logic in Computer Science (Asilomar, CA)*, pages 14–23. IEEE Computer Society Press, June 1989.

[80] Frank J. Oles. *A Category-Theoretic Approach to the Semantics of Programming Languages*. PhD thesis, Syracuse University, 1982.

[81] Frank J. Oles. Type algebras, functor categories, and block structure. In Maurice Nivat and John C. Reynolds, editors, *Algebraic Methods in Semantics*. Cambrige University Press, 1985.

[82] David Pitt. Categories. In Pitt et al. [83], pages 6–15.

[83] David Pitt, Samson Abramsky, Axel Poigne, and David Rydeheard, editors. *Category Theory and Computer Programming (Guildford, U.K.)*, number 240 in Lecture Notes in Computer Science. Springer-Verlag, September 1985.

[84] D. H. Pitt, D. E. Rydeheard, P. Dybjer, A. M. Pitts, and A. Poigne, editors. *Category Theory and Computer Science (Manchester, U.K.)*, number 389 in Lecture Notes in Computer Science. Springer-Verlag, September 1989.

[85] G. D. Plotkin. A powerdomain construction. *SIAM Journal on Computing*, 5(3):452–487, 1976.

[86] Gordon Plotkin. Domains. Lecture notes, Department of Computer Science, University of Edinburgh, 1980.

[87] John Reynolds. Using category theory to design implicit conversions and generic operators. In N. D. Jones, editor, *Proceedings of the Aarhus Workshop on Semantics-Directed Compiler Generation*, number 94 in Lecture Notes in Computer Science. Springer-Verlag, January 1980.

[88] John C. Reynolds. The essence of Algol. In J. W. de Bakker and J. C. van Vliet, editors, *Algorithmic Languages*, pages 345–372, Amsterdam, 1981. North-Holland.

[89] J. C. Reynolds. Polymorphism is not set-theoretic. In G. Kahn, D. B. MacQueen, and G. D. Plotkin, editors, *Semantics of Data Types*, volume 173 of *Lecture Notes in Computer Science*, pages 145–156, Berlin, 1984. Springer-Verlag.

[90] John C. Reynolds. Preliminary design of the programming language Forsythe. Technical Report CMU-CS-88-159, Carnegie Mellon University, June 1988.

[91] John Reynolds. An introduction to the polymorphic lambda calculus. In Huet [51].

[92] John C. Reynolds and Gordon D. Plotkin. On functors expressible in the polymorphic lambda calculus. In Huet [51]. Submitted to Information and Computation. Also available as CMU School of Computer Science technical report number CMU-CS-90-147.

[93] H. E. Rose and J. C. Shepherdson, editors. *Logic Colloquium '73 (Bristol, England)*, number 80 in Studies in Logic and the Foundations of Mathematics. North Holland, 1975.

[94] David Eric Rydeheard. *Applications of Category Theory to Programming and Program Specification*. PhD thesis, University of Edinburgh, 1981. CST-14-81.

[95] David E. Rydeheard. Adjunctions. In Pitt et al. [83], pages 53–57.

[96] David E. Rydeheard. Functors and natural transformations. In Pitt et al. [83], pages 43–52.

[97] D. E. Rydeheard and R. M. Burstall. A categorical unification algorithm. In Pitt et al. [83], pages 493–505.

[98] David E. Rydeheard and Rod M. Burstall. *Computational Category Theory*. Prentice Hall, 1988.

[99] Herbert P. Sander. Categorical combinators. Report 38, Programming Methodology Group, University of Goteborg and Chalmers University of Technology, Sweden, June 1987.

[100] David A. Schmidt. *Denotational Semantics: A Methodology for Language Development*. Allyn and Bacon, 1986.

[101] Horst Schubert. *Categories*. Springer-Verlag, 1972.

[102] Dana Scott. Continuous lattices. In F. W. Lawvere, editor, *Toposes, Algebraic Geometry, and Logic*, number 274 in Lecture Notes in Mathematics, pages 97–136. Springer-Verlag, 1972.

[103] Dana Scott. Data types as lattices. *SIAM Journal on Computing*, 5(3):522–587, 1976.

[104] Dana S. Scott. Relating theories of the λ-calculus. In Seldin and Hindley [108], pages 403–450.

[105] Dana S. Scott. Lectures on a mathematical theory of computation. Technical Report PRG-19, Oxford University, Programming Research Group, May 1981.

[106] Dana S. Scott. Domains for denotational semantics. In M. Nielson and E. M. Schmidt, editors, *Automata, Languages, and Programming: 9th Colloquium, Aarhus, Denmark*, number 140 in Lecture Notes in Computer Science, pages 577–613. Springer-Verlag, 1982.

[107] R. A. G. Seely. Categorical semantics for higher order polymorphic lambda calculus. *Journal of Symbolic Logic*, 52(4):969–988, December 1987.

[108] J. P. Seldin and J. R. Hindley, editors. *To H. B. Curry: Essays on Combinatory Logic, Lambda Calculus and Formalism*. Academic Press, 1980.

[109] M. B. Smyth. Effectively given domains. *Theoretical Computer Science*, 5:257–274, 1977.

[110] M. B. Smyth and G. D. Plotkin. The category-theoretic solution of recursive domain equations. *SIAM Journal on Computing*, 11(4):761–783, 1982.

[111] Joseph E. Stoy. *Denotational Semantics: The Scott-Strachey Approach to Programming Language Theory*. MIT Press, 1977.

[112] A. Tarlecki, R. M. Burstall, and J. A. Goguen. Some fundamental algebraic tools for the semantics of computation: Part III: Indexed categories. Technical Report ECS-LFCS-88-60, Laboratory for Foundations of Computer Science, Department of Computer Science, University of Edinburgh, July 1988. To appear in Theoretical Computer Science.

[113] Alfred Tarski. A lattice-theoretical fixpoint theorem and its applications. *Pacific Journal of Mathematics*, 5:285–309, 1955.

[114] Paul Taylor. *Recursive Domains, Indexed Category Theory, and Polymorphism*. PhD thesis, University of Cambridge, 1986.

[115] R. D. Tennent. Functor-category semantics of programming languages and logics. In Pitt et al. [83], pages 206–224.

[116] James W. Thatcher, Eric G. Wagner, and Jesse B. Wright. Notes on algebraic fundamentals for theoretical computer science. Lecture notes from summer on Foundations of Artificial Intelligence and Computer Science, Pisa, June 1978.

[117] Philip Wadler. Theorems for free! In *Functional Programming Languages and Computer Architecture*, pages 347–359. ACM Press, September 1989. Imperial College, London.

[118] M. Wand. On recursive specification of data types. In Manes [70].

[119] Mitchell Wand. Fixed-point constructions in order-enriched categories. *Theoretical Computer Science*, 8:13–30, 1979.

[120] Glynn Winskel. Categories of models for concurrency. In S. D. Brookes, A. W. Roscoe, and G. Winskel, editors, *Seminar on Concurrency*, number 197 in Lecture Notes in Computer Science, pages 246–267. Springer-Verlag, July 1984.

[121] J. B. Wright, J. A. Goguen, J. W. Thatcher, and E. G. Wagner. Rational algebraic theories and fixed point solutions. In *Proceedings 17th IEEE Symposium on Foundations of Computer Science*, Houston, Texas, 1976.

[122] Jiří Adámek, Horst Herrlich, and George Strecker. *Abstract and Concrete Categories*. John Wiley and Sons, 1990.

Summary of Notation

Notation	Concept	Page
$\mathbf{C}$	category	1
A	object	1
$f : A \to B$	arrow	1
$f \circ g$	composition	1
id_A	identity arrow	1
$dom\ f,\ cod\ f$	domain and codomain	1
$\mathbf{C}^{op}$	dual category	8
$\mathbf{C} \times \mathbf{D}$	product category	9
(A, B)	object of product category	9
(f, g)	arrow of product category	9
$\mathbf{C}^{\to}$	arrow category	9
$\mathbf{D}^{\mathbf{C}}$	functor category	43
0	initial object	16
1	terminal object	16
$!$	unique arrow	16
$A \times B$	product object	18
π_1, π_2	projections	18
$\langle f, g \rangle : C \to A \times B$	mediating arrow to a product	18
$f \times g : A \times B \to C \times D$	arrow between product objects	19
$\prod_{i \in S} A_i$	indexed product	19
π_j	projections	19
$A + B$	coproduct object	19
ι_1, ι_2	injections	19
$[f, g] : A + B \to C$	mediating arrow from a coproduct	19
B^A	exponential object	34
$eval : B^A \times A \to B$	evaluation arrow	34
$curry(g)$	currying	34

Notation	Concept	Page
$F : \mathbf{C} \to \mathbf{D}$	functor	36
$I_{\mathbf{C}}$	identity functor	37
U	forgetful functor	37
Δ	diagonal functor	38
Π	product functor	49
$\mathbf{C}(-,-)$	hom-functor	39
$[- \to -]$	hom-functor (alternative notation)	68
$\tau : F \xrightarrow{\cdot} G$	natural transformation	42
$\tau_A : F(A) \to G(A)$	component of natural transform	42
$f^{\#}$	homomorphic extension of f	45

Index

The MIT Press, with Peter Denning as general consulting editor, publishes computer science books in the following series:

ACM Doctoral Dissertation Award and Distinguished Dissertation Series

Artificial Intelligence
Patrick Winston, Founding editor
Michael Brady, Daniel Bobrow, and Randall Davis, editors

Charles Babbage Institute Reprint Series for the History of Computing
Martin Campbell-Kelly, editor

Computer Systems
Herb Schwetman, editor

Explorations with Logo
E. Paul Goldenberg, editor

Foundations of Computing
Michael Garey and Albert Meyer, editors

History of Computing
I. Bernard Cohen and William Aspray, editors

Information Systems
Michael Lesk, editor

Logic Programming
Ehud Shapiro, editor; Fernando Pereira, Koichi Furukawa, Jean-Louis Lassez, and David H. D. Warren, Associate editors

The MIT Press Electrical Engineering and Computer Science Series

Research Monographs in Parallel and Distributed Processing
Christopher Jesshope and David Klappholz, editors

Scientific and Engineering Computation
Janusz Kowalik, editor

Technical Communication
Ed Barrett, editor